The Logic of Human Personality

The Logic of
Human Personality

An Onto-Logical Account

Mary L. O'Hara

HUMANITIES PRESS
NEW JERSEY

First published in 1997 by
Humanities Press International, Inc.
165 First Avenue, Atlantic Highlands, New Jersey 07716

© 1997 by Mary L. O'Hara

Library of Congress Cataloging-in-Publication Data
O'Hara, Mary Louise R.
    The logic of human personality : an onto-logical account / Mary
Louise O'Hara.
      p. cm.
    Includes bibliographical references and index.
    ISBN 0-391-04022-7
    1. Agent (Philosophy)—History. 2. Personality—Philosophy—
History. I. Title.
BD450.O376   1997
126—DC21   96-39586
                                            CIP

Printed in the United States of America

To my sister
Eileen O'Hara Lexau
and
to the memory
of our brothers
and our parents,
Louise M. (Triska)
and
James H. O'Hara
who taught us
to value learning
and, most of all,
devotion.

Contents

Preface   ix
Acknowledgments   xi

Introduction   The Human Person: A Logical/Historical Study   1

Part 1   Objections to the Traditional Notion of Person

1   Mill and Other Critics of the Categories   10
2   Dewey's Dissatisfaction   18
3   Marcel's Philosophy of the Person   30

Part 2   A History of the Notion of Person

4   Ancient Sources of the Word 'Person'   42
5   Medieval and Early Modern Views of Person   53
6   The Vanishing Person: The *Encyclopaedia Britannica*   67

Part 3   An Onto-Logical Account of the Person

7   An Individual Substance   80
8   Quality and the Rational Nature   89
9   Quantity, Place, and Position as Personal Categories   98
10   Persons in Relationships   104
11   Action, Passion, and the Compassionate Buddha   110
12   Persons in Time   119
13   The Category of "Having" as Revealing the Person   127

Conclusion   135

Appendix: Personalisms   139
Select Bibliography   143
Index   145

Preface

In writing this book I have had in mind students and others who may find in it answers to questions they and I have had, and also a stimulus to continue the discussion and research needed to bring light to bear upon the important question of the nature of human personality.

To the many persons who have helped bring this work to completion, I am most grateful. My late colleague, Annette Walters, C.S.J., first suggested the topic of the person as an object of research and encouraged me to pursue it.

Madonna R. Adams has given continuing enthusiastic support and assistance in research, in reading the manuscript in preliminary versions, in discussions, and in editing it in its final form.

Walter H. Principe, C.S.B., and Dolores Steinberg read the entire manuscript and offered encouragement and criticism helpful in revising it. Others who read parts of it and offered suggestions for its improvement were William Baumgaertner; Vincent Colapietro; Susan L. Krantz; Catherine Lexau; the late John H. Nota, S. J.; and Robert J. Roth, S. J.

At various critical points in its development, the following persons gave welcome assistance: Monika Asztolos; Seth Benardete; John J. Conley, S. J.; Ewert Cousins; Robert Cummings Neville; Anita Pampusch; A. J. Rist; William A. Wallace, O.P.; and the late James A. Weisheipl, O. P. For help with computer problems, I am grateful to M. R. Grady, C.S.J., and Cynthia L. Krey.

Finally, I am grateful to the members of my religious community for their support during the time I have devoted to this work, and in particular to Ann V. Walton, C.S.J.

Acknowledgments

Permission has been granted to reprint from *The Collected Works of John Dewey*, ed. JoAnn Boydston. © Copyright by The Board of Trustees, Southern Illinois University, published with permission of the publisher Southern Illinois University Press.

I am grateful to the Messenger Press for permission to publish a revised version of the article on "Marcel's Concept of Person," originally published in *Philosophy Today*, Vol. 8, nn. 3–4 (Fall 1964): 147–54, and to *International Studies in Philosophy* for permission to publish a revised form of "The Vanishing Person," which appeared in Vol. 27, n. 2 (1995): 101–107.

Permission has been granted by Editions Gallimard, Paris, for quotations from Gabriel Marcel, *Creative Fidelity*, trans. Robert Rosthal, published by The Noonday Press, 1964, © Editions Gallimard, 1940.

Introduction
The Human Person:
A Logical/Historical Study

A Person is an individual substance of a rational nature.

—Boethius

A Hermeneutic for the Study of Personhood

Today, most philosophical writing about the person deals with personal identity. This has been true since the time of John Locke (1632–1704).[1] Logically, however, a prior question is: What does 'person' mean? It is this question, in its historical settings, that the present work considers.

Identity of Dolls, Nature of Persons

In my own case, concern for identity preceded that for person. I must have been three-and-a-half or so, living in a world of knees, skirts, trouser-legs, and two older brothers, dragging my constant companion, a worn-out doll, everywhere, to the amusement of everyone. It defined my world. Nothing my brothers said about it could bring me to part with it. Then one night it disappeared. When I realized it was gone, I looked for it everywhere and asked everyone about it again and again, heartsick at its loss.

I did notice a conspiratorial air hovering about the place; I was met with looks I had never seen before, knowing and mischievous looks from my brothers. On Christmas, as I opened my first present, I noticed everyone watching me. The package contained a doll, brightly painted and dressed in new clothes. I looked at the little newcomer, but I could not bring myself to let it into my still insecure world. Everyone said, "It's your doll, repainted!" I remembered

1

my doll, but something in my stomach did not recognize this doll as identically the same. It was a stranger, with no claim on my interest or affection.

I knew nothing of Plato's ship, rebuilt plank by plank until it was essentially a completely new entity, while still being thought of as the same boat. I could not have expressed it then, but the identity of the doll was what was in question.

My interest in the nature of persons developed later, when, as an adolescent reading Arthur Conan Doyle's theosophical literature, I realized that I was searching for something hard and permanent, perhaps what Gerard Manley Hopkins called "immortal diamond."[2]

Given the opportunity to study psychology in an atmosphere, in Minnesota in the '40s, characterized by a strong interest in Logical Positivism and the foundations of scientific knowledge, I preferred to do graduate work in philosophy. It was Herbert Feigl who later advised me to study the *word* 'person' as a means to understanding persons in reality. And finally, collaborating with a colleague in writing a book on *Persons and Personality*,[3] I came away with numerous questions and few answers.

These then, are some of the sources of an abiding interest in persons, and in how 'person' should be defined, that has characterized my adult years.

DRAWING DEFINING LINES

To define is to "draw the line," to set limits to the use of a term, to circumscribe its use for a particular purpose, as a scientific term, for example. Still, few individuals enjoy the privilege of establishing the meaning of words: the way the word is used by those who speak the language, what philosophers have come to call "ordinary language," in the end determines how it will be understood.

But since there is a reciprocal influence between ordinary and scientific language, it is important in some cases to be aware of the different usages. Such is surely the case with the word 'person'. A word in ordinary use, it has a long and complex history.

PLACE, TIME, PERSON

For over 2,000 years some human beings have called themselves persons, and a few have speculated about just what this means. The notion of being a person figures prominently in Western thought from the time of Cicero (106–43 B.C.E.) and earlier; it does not seem to have been a theme of discussion in the Orient.[4]

Philosophers and theologians, linguists and jurists have seen the person in a variety of ways, depending upon their particular interests. Since the word 'person' is found in ordinary as well as legal language, in recent years philosophers and experts on law as well as ordinary people have debated the question of what constitutes human personality.

Even in its earliest use, the word connoted dignity. In ancient Rome the free male citizen was able to function in public life in ways women or slaves could not: Roman law defined persons and their privileges. In the Greek-speaking world, the word bore a more physical connotation, having come from the word for 'face' (*prosopon*). These different connotations are to be found in the use of the word today.

Today, however, most philosophers who write about the nature of human personality put forth their ideas in a Cartesian context, seeing the human being as an uneasy combination of mental and physical characteristics. They ask whether the human person is a purely spiritual or perhaps a completely material being. Thus the question of the nature of personal identity comes down to specifying what characteristics shall be regarded as essential to this individual person. Should persistent memories or rather an intact brain (or finger- or voice-prints, for example) be taken as the proper criterion for the reidentification of a person? The history of the use of the word goes back far beyond the modern period however; it is thus important to consider how it was used a millenium and a half before Descartes (1596–1650).

The contexts in which 'person' has been used have changed over the millenia; and its meanings have developed differently in various languages. In particular, the philosophical contexts in which the word has been used have varied, from a strongly theological background in Boethius (ca. 480–524, author of the first recorded definition of the meaning of the word) to a number of psychological and anthropological vocabularies today. An attempt to understand the meaning of 'person' in its historical setting prompts the present approach to the question of the nature of human personality. To try to gain control of the meaning of this word over the last two millenia, then, we ask: What is the nature of the logic governing the use of the word 'person'? To discern the logical constraints governing the use of the term today, it is useful to look at the history of the word, as it has come into such modern languages as English and French, and to try to determine what factors may have caused it to be used differently at various times.[5]

Boethius's definition of the word 'person' used an expression that seems to refer to the philosophy of Aristotle (384–322 B.C.E.), "individual substance." Even though Aristotle's extant works have nothing to say about personhood as such, therefore, to understand the history of the word involves getting acquainted with Aristotle's logical works. These comprise modes of reasoning not limited to the syllogistic method, and they embrace presyllogistic discussion of definition and division. In particular they involve the categories and the predicables.

Aristotle's *Categories* constituted the essential foundation of a great scheme of scientific research the like of which has never been set up by any other thinker. It lists uses of words to be found in the predicates of simple declarative sentences called "propositions." If the sentence says, "John is a man," the word 'man' is put into the category of "substance." In "John is white," the predicate, 'white', is put into the "accidental" category of "quality."

BOETHIUS, MACMURRAY, KANT: PERSONS AS SUFFERING

Boethius's definition of 'person' as "an individual substance of a rational nature"[6] invites comparison with contrasting notions of persons as related and active. This distinction between substance and its "accidents" of relation and action in reference to the person is fundamentally important to understanding the nature of human personhood in its historical setting.

John Macmurray, in his Gifford Lectures, argued for the central importance of *acting* and of *relationship* as criteria of personhood.[7] While it is true, however, that agency points to the very core of human personality, it is equally necessary to examine the meaning of the person as patient—receiver of action. In Roman law, the person is one capable of acting in a legal capacity: slaves are not persons in this sense. But another side of human reality is that of suffering, of receiving action from outside oneself, and this points more to the material aspect of the human being than to the capable, adult, generally male, individual. The developing fetus (that can nevertheless make its mark through a blood type different from its mother's, for example) or the senile or comatose person whose vulnerability is the quality most visible to observers, can manifest the receiving aspect of human personality most clearly. Not just the young and the old and the infirm, however, but every human being needs society, with its give and take, to live humanly. "Man," says Aristotle, "is naturally a political animal."[8] Human beings can develop properly only in a social setting; a child brought up in total isolation is permanently crippled as a human being.

Buddhist meditation practice seems directed toward heightened awareness of one's perceptions, so as to eliminate through manipulation of one's mental powers the perception of suffering (although the Buddha, like other Oriental thinkers, was apparently interested less in the theoretical than in the practical, and so differs from the Western thinkers in question here). The German philosopher Immanuel Kant (1724–1804), on the other hand, seems to have despaired of complete self-possession. His criticism of human knowledge, as this was discussed by Locke and later English thinkers, in large measure set the stage for discussion of the person in the past two centuries. The "noumenal ego" Kant postulated is by definition ultimately unknowable.[9]

DIFFICULTIES

When Boethius defined 'person' using the expression 'individual substance', he seems to have intended to state what Aristotle meant by the technical term 'first substance'.[10] After centuries of scientific literature dealing with "chemical substances," and in a time of "controlled substances," it is difficult, today, to return to the world of Aristotle where 'substance' refers not to palpable matter, nor even to the impalpable prime matter postulated to underly every material thing, but rather to a mode of being: being able to exist on its own, not as a necessary mode or aspect of another.[11] If we are to make sense of the notion of person as this has come down to us from Boethius, therefore, a return to the ancient world is essential.

One of the first things that strikes a reader of Aristotle is that his philosophical library features logic in its first six books. This is fitting, inasmuch as Aristotle seems to have been the first Western thinker to see logic as the universal tool of science. The first Aristotelian logical work is the *Categories*, the work from which Boethius no doubt took the notion of individual or "first" substance: this man or this horse, as distinct from a "secondary" substance like the idea of humanity, an idea realized at no time in history, but standing for all human beings, whenever they exist.

The *Categories*[12] is a difficult, much commented upon book that has been praised, criticized, and, by John Stuart Mill and others, scorned during the almost 2,500 years it has existed. The reasons for the disfavor into which it has fallen are various, and some will be considered in what follows. Whether the categories are to be taken in a merely logical sense (as referring to the predicates of simple propositions) or also in a metaphysical sense (as indicating the objects denoted by these predicates) is a much discussed question with metaphysical implications that need not be considered here. Does the word 'man' in "John is a man" refer to the species man, humanity, alone, or also to this individual human being here and now?[13] Some thinkers today see the use of the category of "substance" in Boethius's definition as making the definition outdated. Their reason seems to be that they see substance as necessarily rigid and reified, "thingified," and one might say made too concrete and material. As noted above, this prejudice on the part of readers in recent centuries may result from incautiously reading today's ordinary meanings back into technical terms that look the same but have a quite distinct and limited sense. The change in meaning can in any case lead to confusion and even to complete misunderstanding.[14]

Despite these difficulties, it seems important, in the interest of gaining an understanding of how the word 'person' enters into discussion today, to be guided by the ten categories. Although these categories have occasioned considerable debate over the millenia, their meaning in a general sense is sufficiently clear to allow them to serve as guideposts for the present undertaking.[15]

The present work, while it is concerned with historical questions, gets its primary structure from the ten categories. In the spirit of Aristotle's dialectic, it opens with a first part intended to bring the question to a focus through a discussion of objections to the categories as they have come down to us. Some questions raised by modern and recent thinkers about Greek philosophy, the categories, and substance are considered first: Chapter 1 deals with criticisms of the categories. Chapters 2 and 3 treat of two twentieth-century thinkers who endeavored to understand the notion of human personality in reference to ancient sources of information about the words 'person' and 'substance'.[16] Part 2 discusses the earlier history of the use of the word; and Part 3 attempts to show how the categories, in particular those of substance, quality, relation, and action, contribute to an appreciation of the meaning of the nature of human personality today.

In light of the considerable amounts of contemporary literature available on the subject of the person, the works chosen for discussion here are principally those that take account of the ancient sources of the word 'person', or that refer to non-Western notions of personhood.

NOTES

1. For a discussion of Locke's idea of person, see Jenny Teichman, "The Definition of Person," *Philosophy*, 60, no. 232 (April 1985): 175–185, for example, 179: "Much recent philosophy, . . . if put into legislation, would have the effect of reducing the area of rights by reducing the number of human beings who count as persons. . . ." And 180: "It seems obvious that Boethius' definition must have percolated down to Locke." And finally, 182: ". . . no [individual Lockean] person can lack consciousness or memory for even one moment." Locke's "person" is described below in Chapter 6.

2. Gerard Manley Hopkins, *A Hopkins Reader*, ed. John Pick (New York: Doubleday & Company, Image Books Edition, 1966), 80–81: "That nature is a Heraclitean Fire and of the Comfort of the Resurrection."

3. Annette Walters with M. [L.] O'Hara (New York: Appleton Century Crofts, 1953).

4. In the *Bhagavad Gita*, when Arjuna recoils from battle against his own kin, his divine charioteer explains to him that the only real actor is Brahman; all human beings can do is enter into what has been divinely decreed and will be carried out by divine power. The notion of person as agent would not readily emerge from such a background. Fustel de Coulanges, *The Ancient City* (Baltimore: The Johns Hopkins University Press, 1980), 103, n. 16, speaks of a time when the notion of the individual person did not figure prominently in Western thought, either: "For the old domestic religion, the family was the true body, of which the individual was but an inseparable member; the patronymic was, therefore, the first name in date and in importance. The new religion, on the contrary, recognized in the individual complete liberty and entire personal independence, . . . Baptismal names were, therefore, the first, and for a long time the only, names."

    Derek Parfit, *Reasons and Persons* (Oxford: Oxford University Press, 1984), argues for treating persons as aggregates like nations, rather than as [Cartesian] "separately existing entities" (273). He likens his view to an Eastern opinion that there is no persisting person, saying "*Buddha would have agreed*." Teichman, "Definition," 1985, finds that Locke's "concept of a person is more like the concept of a state than the concept of a thing. Personhood in Locke's *Essay* is more like *being magnetized* than like *being iron*" (180). On the need to recognize and describe rather than prescribe and construct what persons are, see David Wiggins, "Personal Identity," in *Sameness and Substance* (Oxford: Basil Blackwell, 1980): "Let us rewrite Locke's famous sentence, and say that a person is any animal the physical make-up of whose species constitutes the species' typical members thinking intelligent beings. . . ." (188). See also Wiggins's "The Person as Object of Science, as Subject of Experience, and as

Locus of Value," in Arthur Peacocke and Grant Gillett, eds., *Persons and Personality: A Contemporary Inquiry* (Oxford: Basil Blackwell, 1987): "A person is a creature with whom we can get onto terms, or a creature that is of the same animal nature and psychological makeup as creatures with whom we can get onto terms, there being no clear limit to how far the process can go." (72)

5. Catherine McCall, *The Concept of Person: An Analysis of Concepts of Person, Self, and Human Being* (Brookfield, VT: Gower Publishing Company, 1990) offers a survey of contemporary literature on the nature of the person to 1985.

6. Boethius, *A Treatise against Eutyches and Nestorius*, III, in *The Theological Tractates*, trans. H. F. Stewart and E. K. Rand (New York: G. P. Putnam's Sons, 1926), 85.

7. *Persons in Relation* (Atlantic Highlands, NJ: Humanities Press International, 1991); *The Self as Agent* (Atlantic Highlands, NJ: Humanities Press International, 1991). The word 'personality' in the present work is generally used as equivalent to 'personhood', for that which makes a person to be a person; it does not have the meaning of the psychological term in a phrase like 'personality assessment'.

8. *Aristotle's Politics*, trans. H. G. Apostle (Grinnell, IA: The Peripatetic Press, 1986), 1.2.1253a3. *Aristotle's Nicomachean Ethics*, trans. H. G. Apostle (The Peripatetic Press, 1984), 9.9.1169b18.

9. Aristotle hovers in the background of the treatment of the categories in Kant's *Critique of Pure Reason*, trans. Norman Kemp Smith (New York: St. Martin's Press, 1929). But in reference to Aristotle, Kant's attitude seems ambivalent; he respects Aristotle's search for categories, but considers it "rhapsodic"—purely haphazard, and confused: to his original ten categories, Kant says, he adds postpredicaments like motion.

Kant appears to have studied the various parts of Aristotle's logic, including the *Topics*, and perhaps to have modeled his "analytic" upon that of the Stagirite, and his "dialectic" upon that of Plato and of Aristotle. He gives no evidence of having read Aristotle's *Physics*, although he treats matters like the notion of chance and the distinction between mathematics and natural science in the first *Critique*. For Kant, the self, along with the world and God, are Ideas, which by definition cannot be known as they really are. See *Critique of Pure Reason*, Transcendental Analytic, Sec. 3, "Categories," B105–09 (113–15 in Smith). And, on person, Transcendental Dialectic, Bk. II, Chapter I. "The Paralogisms of Pure Reason," A361–66 (341–45 in Smith).

10. *Aristotle's Categories and Propositions*, trans. Hippocrates G. Apostle (Grinnell, IA: The Peripatetic Press, 1980), 5.2a12–14.

11. For some recent treatments of Aristotle's substance doctrine, see M. L. O'Hara, ed., *Substances and Things* (Lanham, MD: University Press of America, 1982).

12. For some, the *Categories* (hereafter: *Cat.*), on account of its abrupt beginning and other characteristics, is a doubtfully Aristotelian work.

13. See Steven K. Strange, "Plotinus, Porphyry, and the Neoplatonic Interpretation of the 'Categories'," pp. 955–74 in *Aufsteig und Niedergang der Römischen Welt* (hereafter: ANRW), eds. W. Haase and Hildegard Temporini, Part II: Principat, Vol. 36: 2 *Philosophie (Platonismus) Aristotelismus* (New York: 1987): "Whereas Porphyry claims that the 'Categories' is a purely logical work, his master Plotinus takes it to be a work of metaphysics" (964). "Simplicius, following Porphyry, gives the defense of Aristotle's 'Categories' on the grounds that Aristotle knows that language is primarily about sensibles, and ignores intelligibles . . . because . . . they cannot be spoken about without shifting the normal meanings of words. . . ." (974). H. B. Gottschalk, "Aristotelian philosophy in the Roman World from the time of

Cicero to the end of the second century AD," 1079–1174, in the same volume, relates the history of commentaries on the *Categories* in the early centuries of our era. "All these efforts were summed up in the great commentaries of Alexander of Aphrodisias and Porphyry; through the latter this work . . . became one of the basic philosophical texts of the Middle Ages" (1102).

14. A different sort of objection was made by Russell, *My Philosophical Development* (New York: 1959), 135, (cited in Roderick Chisholm, *Person and Object: A Metaphysical Study* (London: George Allen and Unwin, 1976), 197, n. 5: "'The subject, however, appears to be a logical fiction, like mathematical points and instants.'" Chisholm effectively refutes this claim and concludes that "Our definition . . . would seem to be equivalent in intent to that proposed by Boethius: A person is an individual substance of a rational nature." See also Bernard Lonergan, *The Subject* (Milwaukee: Marquette University Press, 1968); and, on Lonergan's "subject," Eugene Webb, *Philosophers of Consciousness* (Seattle: University of Washington Press, 1988), 84–90.

15. Marcel Mauss in his last essay, "A Category of the Human Mind: the Notion of Person; The Notion of Self," trans. W. D. Halls, in Michael Carrithers, et al., *The Category of the Person: Anthropology, Philosophy, History* (Cambridge: Cambridge University Press, 1985), speaks of the usefulness of the Aristotelian categories for anthropological research among certain tribal groups.

16. For a metaphysical discussion of some of the questions here considered principally from a logical or natural point of view, see W. Norris Clarke, S. J., *Person and Being* (Milwaukee: Marquette University Press, 1993). For an analysis of the various uses of 'person' in philosophy today and in the recent past, see Amélie O. Rorty, "Persons and *Personae*," in Christopher Gill, ed., *The Person and the Human Mind: Issues in Ancient and Modern Philosophy* (Oxford: Clarendon Press, 1990), 21–38.

PART 1

Objections to the
Traditional Notion
of Person

The concept of "person" is not only a marvelous theory; it is at the center of the human *ethos*.

—John Paul II

Part 1 of this work focuses on the question of the nature of human personhood by taking up objections offered by various recent thinkers to the notion of person as defined in traditional philosophies from ancient times.

The first chapter considers objections to the idea of categorization, often seen by modern thinkers as too outdated, nonpersonal, or trivial.

Chapters 2 and 3 take up twentieth-century thinkers, the American John Dewey and the French existentialist Gabriel Marcel, who tried to understand the notion of human personhood and made it central to their respective systems of thought. Each of them brought his own point of view to bear upon the notion of person, but neither succeeded in explaining it to his own satisfaction.

1

Mill and Other Critics
of the Categories

Opposing Aristotle's logic is like opposing the multiplication tables.

—G. K. Chesterton

STEWART'S DIFFICULTIES

To understand the earliest recorded definition of 'person', it is essential to understand Aristotle's categories.[1] But coming to such an understanding is not easy for a number of reasons. For one thing the very question of what the categories are meant to categorize has been disputed.[2] In addition, the ten categories form a disparate list of items. This has puzzled some thinkers and led others to think the whole notion of the categories is ill-conceived.

The Scottish philosopher Dugald Stewart (1753–1828) is an example of the latter group. In a dissertation meant to bring up to date the *Encyclopaedia Britannica*'s sixth edition, he poured his scorn upon those who emphasize the need to study Aristotle's categories:

> In consequence of the stress laid on *predicaments*, men came to imagine, that to know the nature of anything, it is sufficient to know under what *predicament* or *category* it ought to be arranged; . . .[3]

In so doing, Stewart says, they were influenced by the old scholastic usage, which took the word 'substance' to correspond to "the Greek word *ousia*, as employed by Aristotle to denote the first of the predicaments; . . ." This usage differed from the popular use of 'substance' for something material.

But, Stewart notes,

> [t]he Greek word *ousia* . . . is not liable to these objections. It obtrudes no sensible image on the fancy; and, in this respect, has a great advantage over the Latin word *substantia*. The former, in its logical acceptation, is an extension to Matter, of an idea originally derived from Mind. The latter is an

10

extension to Mind, of an idea originally derived from Matter.

Instead of defining *mind* [after Descartes's example] to be a thinking *substance*, it seems much more logically correct to define it as a thinking *being*.[4]

Stewart strove to bring philosophic usage out of an earlier time, when, for instance, Thomas Hobbes (1588–1679) could speak of metaphysics or

philosophia prima on which all other Philosophy ought to depend: and [which] consisteth principally in right limiting of the significance of such appellations, or names as are . . . the most universal [and] . . . serve to avoid ambiguity or equivocation . . . [and] are called Definitions; such as are the Definitions of Body, . . . Matter, . . . Subject, Substance, Accident . . . and divers others. . . .[5]

When Stewart was writing, Hobbes's list was "no longer to be heard of, even in the walls of our universities," having been replaced by ethical, critical, and philological enquiries, as well as "inductive philosophy of the human mind" and speculation about mathematics and physics. Stewart rejoiced in what he regarded as this progress of the human mind, convinced as he was that "the discovery of philosophical truth . . . always adds to the sum of human happiness."[6] Kant's categories, constructed on a different principle from those of Aristotle, were no more acceptable to Stewart than Aristotle's.

MILL'S QUESTIONS

The English philosopher John Stuart Mill (1806–73) wrote an influential work on logic published in 1843. Like his Scottish predecessor Stewart, he saw little merit in Aristotle's categories, and in fact despaired of making sense out of them.

Despite his intent to accommodate as much of traditional logic as possible, he found some aspects of Aristotle's theory of little use. In the Preface to his *System of Logic*, he says:

. . . many useful principles and distinctions which were contained in the old Logic, have been gradually omitted from the writings of its later teachers; . . . it appeared desirable both to revive these and to reform and rationalize the philosophical foundation on which they stood. The earlier chapters of this preliminary Book will consequently appear, to some readers, needlessly elementary and scholastic. But those who know in what darkness the nature of our knowledge, and of the processes by which it is obtained, is often involved by a confused apprehension of the import of the different classes of Words and Assertions, will not regard these discussions as either frivolous, or irrelevant to the topics considered in the later Books.[7]

Mill later lists, in Greek and Latin, the ten categories of Aristotle (although in a different order from Aristotle's list in *Categories*)[8] from *ousia* or *substantia* to *echein* or *habitus*. Of these he says:

The imperfections of this classification are too obvious to require, and its merits not sufficient to reward, a minute examination. It is a mere catalogue of the distinctions rudely marked out by the language of familiar life, with little or no attempt to penetrate, by philosophic analysis, to the *rationale* even of these common distinctions. Such an analysis, however superficially conducted, would have shown the enumeration to be both redundant and defective. Some objects are omitted, and others repeated several times under different heads. . . . The incongruity of erecting into a *summum genus* the class which forms the tenth category is manifest.[9]

The tenth category in Mill's listing is that of clothing or possession.

What are these Aristotelian categories that are treated with such disdain by Mill and Stewart?[10]

ARISTOTLE'S CATEGORIES

Aristotle's theory of the categories—or classes of predicates of sentences—can be seen as merely logical or also as metaphysical. The predicate of a simple declarative sentence expressing a judgment can refer to (and so be called) a substance or else some modification of a substance.

According to Aristotle, a substance can, generally speaking, be modified in nine ways: in reference to its quantity, quality, relation, where, when, posture, clothing, action, and passion (that is, being acted upon).[11] These modifications of substances are called 'accidents'. 'Accident' is a technical term that derives from the Latin and indicates something contingent or dependent upon something else. Aristotle's "accidents" are so called because by their very notion, they inhere in something that exists in or through itself: color inheres in wood as the quality of the substance of wood.

In setting up a theory of the existence of substances, Aristotle effects an economy in explanation: he is able to dispense with the myriad entities that would emerge as quasi-substances (as "things") were they not relegated to the status of accidents—of inherent beings, dependent upon that in which they inhere. In this way he avoids the false reification, the over realization, of entities that merely pertain to things without being themselves things in the full sense. Abhorrence of a scientifically unproductive infinite regress in explanation and of the absurdity of multiplying entities beyond necessity would impel Aristotle to posit substances.[12] These ten classes of predicates, substance and the nine accidents, are what are meant by Aristotle's categories, and, importantly for the discussion that follows, are also referred to as the ten *predicaments*.

PREDICABLES

To be distinguished from the categories (or predicaments, as they are sometimes called) are the five "predicables."[13] The "predicables" are classes of logical *relations* between subject (S) and predicate (P) in a sentence. This relation may be necessary (as in a definition) or necessarily implied (that is, a "property"), or merely "accidental," so called because of the contingent relation between a given predicate and the subject of the sentence.[14] The relations between subject and predicate in a simple proposition can be illustrated in a chart of the five PREDICABLES:

P is related to S:
   essentially, either as $\left\{\begin{array}{l}\textit{genus}\\ \text{or}\\ [\textit{species}] \text{ (the species being}\\ \text{differentiated from the genus by the}\end{array}\right.$

or   *specific difference)*

   nonessentially, as $\left\{\begin{array}{l}\textit{property}\\ \text{or}\\ \textit{accident}\end{array}\right.$

As an example of these relations one may take that of "rational animal" considered as an essential definition of the human being: 'animal' is the genus, 'rational' is the specific difference, and the two words together designate the "species." "Risibility," or ability to laugh, is generally taken to be a necessarily implied "property" of every human being, with a quality like "hungry" or "redheaded" being called "accidental." A quality like "redheaded," for example, can change without a change in the definition of the human being, when the redheaded person becomes grey.

It is important to notice that the predicables, in being classes of relations between words, have to do first of all with such mentally existing entities as definitions. In no sense can these mental relations as such be considered real things: they are convenient tools with which one can consider mental entities. A red pencil (with its substantial wood and accidental color) may roll off a desk; a definition can never do so. One need not, indeed must not, read back into reality the purely logical requirements of definitions. The word 'accident', then, means something different when used of predicamental (categorical) accidents from what it does when used of predicable accidents.

PREDICATES: PREDICAMENTS AND PREDICABLES

Since the technical terms, 'predicaments' and 'predicables' refer to two distinct types of analyses, 'accident' or 'accidental' with reference to a class of relations in the predicables is not to be confused with 'accident' referring to one of the nine categories or predicaments. The word 'accident' means something different when used of predicamental (categorical) accidents from what it does when it is used of predicable accidents. Thus, to confuse the predicable 'accident' with the predicamental or categorical 'accidents' would no doubt involve the worst sort of category mistake.

CATEGORIES AS MANIFESTING THE STRUCTURE OF THE WORLD

The view that the structure of the world is made manifest in the categories has been discussed and disputed innumerable times since Aristotle. At the macroscopic level, the level at which "man is the measure of all," clearly observable articulations do exist: Inuit people are said to have words to distinguish a score of different kinds of snow.[15] Human beings seem to need to categorize; no doubt the world may be cut up differently for a number of different purposes, as the sun's rays can be made to appear different through the use of different filters. Practical aims influence ways of categorizing; furthermore, metaphysical presuppositions may influence one's way of seeing those suggested long ago by Aristotle.[16]

The *Categories* of Aristotle represents a first attempt to expose systematically the joints in reality, to discover how the world is put together in relation to human knowledge and human language. To say that science necessarily begins at the human level is not to judge whether or not knowledge at this level will be found in the last analysis to be the most intellectually satisfying. What is most intelligible in itself is not necessarily so for us.[17] To understand the Ptolemaic and also the Copernican universes is to know something of a rough mathematical parallel between two possible systems of moving bodies. It is also to appreciate the importance of point of view in relation to human knowledge. Most of all, perhaps, it is to realize what it means for a human being to be earth-bound as distinguished from being a traveller in space: being in space and observing the universe from there is no doubt the best way to come to know the universe as it is. But astronomical numbers of calculations are required to put a human being safely into space.

Aristotle assumes the existence of substances in the natural world. In the initial dialectic introducing his *Physics*, he makes it clear that to deny the existence of changing things in the world, as the pre-Socratic philosophers Parmenides and Melissus did, is to render scientific investigation unthinkable.[18]

Numerous thinkers in modern times have found Aristotle's theory of substance unsatisfactory. From the point of view of economy, however, the theory of substance still has much to recommend it, since it is no less probable and no more cumbersome than competing Platonist or reifying theories. And, as the contemporary thinker P. F. Strawson[19] has made clear, it is in any case embedded in contemporary English.

OBJECTIONS FROM THEOLOGIANS

A typically twentieth-century objection to Aristotle's category of substance is put forward by theologians who see it as too material to be applied to human life or to anything living. In particular, the German theologians Michael Schmaus and Heribert Mühlen object to the use of 'substance' in defining 'person': The categories elaborated by Aristotle "correspond to the being of nature, but not to the being of the person."[20] This objection seems to assume a division between person and nature, setting the person over against nature; but surely one cannot be a human person without a human nature, subject to the natural laws that govern all natural entities.

The French philosopher Gabriel Marcel made a similar criticism of the Aristotelian notion of substance as being too "*chosist*" or thingified to be useful in talking about persons. Marcel's position is considered in detail in Chapter 3.

CONCLUSION

The categories were not used by Aristotle himself to analyze the notion of human personality. In spite of the many attacks upon the categories, and particularly that of substance, however, the present work aims to show that these tools of thinking offer a valid and useful way of organizing speculation about persons. Above all they are essential for understanding the debates about human personality that have occurred over the centuries.

NOTES

1. The definition is that of Boethius, in his *Treatise against Eutyches and Nestorius*, II–III; see the Introduction, above.
2. Some recent editions and discussions of the categories include Christos Evangeliou, *Aristotle's Categories and Porphyry* (New York: E. J. Brill, 1988), and *Dexippus On Aristotle's Categories*, trans. John Dillon (Ithaca, NY: Cornell University Press, 1990).
3. *Dissertation Exhibiting the Progress of Metaphysical, Ethical, and Political Philosophy Since the Revival of Letters in Europe*, 2nd ed. (Edinburgh: T. and T. Clark, 1877), "Notes and Illustrations to Dissertation," Part I, n. I, 542 (originally published 1815–1821).
4. Ibid.
5. Ibid. See Thomas Hobbes, *Leviathan* (Oxford: Clarendon Press, 1958; reprinted from the 1651 edition), IV, 46, 523–24.
6. *Dissertation*, III, 521. The Port Royal Logic of Antoine Arnauld (1662) says of the categories: "These are the ten Aristotelian Categories of which so much mystery has been made. To speak the truth, they are in themselves of very little use. . . .

   "The first reason [for the categories' being a hindrance to knowledge] is that these . . . are regarded as being established by reason and by truth, rather than as entirely arbitrary. . . . In fact, the following couplet was devised by the new philosophy [Cartesianism] to exhibit all the possible ways of considering the things in the world:

   > *Mens, mensura, quies, motus, positura, figura,*
   > *Sunt cum materia cunctarum exordia rerum.*
   > Mind, measure, rest, motion, position, shape
   > Are with matter all the kinds of things.

   "The second reason . . . is that the study accustoms men to be satisfied with mere words."—Antoine Arnauld, *The Art of Thinking: Port-Royal Logic*, trans. James

Dickoff and Patricia James (Indianapolis: The Bobbs-Merrill Company, 1964), 43–44, xix. John Locke appears to have used this book.

7. *A System of Logic Ratiocinative and Inductive: Being a Connected View of the Principles of Evidence and the Methods of Scientific Investigation* (Toronto: University of Toronto Press, 1973), p. cxii.

8. "Expressions which are in no way composite signify either a substance, a quantity, or a quality, or a relation, or somewhere, or at some time, or being in a position, or possessing, or acting, or being acted upon." H. G. Apostle, trans., *Aristotle's Categories and Propositions* (Grinnell, IA: The Peripatetic Press, 1980), 4.26–28. Charlotte Stough, in "Language and Ontology in Aristotle's Categories," points out that while "adjectives, adverbs, prepositional phrases and finite forms of verbs" are used to express the nine accidents, "grammatical substantives are reserved for the category of substance." *Journal of the History of Philosophy*, 10, 3 (July 1972): 269.

9. "Of the Things Denoted by Names," *System*, I, 3, 1, p. 47 in the Toronto edition.

10. Michael Novak, "Toward Understanding Aristotle's *Categories*," *Philosophy and Phenomenological Research* 26, 1 (September 1965): 117–120, offers an explanation of the first five chapters of the work.

11. For a list of the categories, see, in addition to Aristotle's *Categories* 4, *Topics* 1.9.103b20–27, *Physics* 5.1.225b5–8, and *Metaphysics* (hereafter: *Met.*) (Z) 7.4.1029b23–25, and, for Aristotle's discussion of some of them from the metaphysical point of view, *Met.* (Delta) 5.8.1017b10–14, 23–25, et passim. On the doctrine of substance, see Joseph Owens, *The Doctrine of Being in the Aristotelian Metaphysics*, 2nd ed. (Toronto: The Pontifical Institute of Mediaeval Studies, 1963); M. L. O'Hara, ed., *Substances*, 1–13, treats of substance principally as it relates to the sciences.

12. See Aristotle *Metaphysics* (M) 13.4.1079a.

13. See St. Thomas Aquinas, *Summa Theologiae*, Latin text and English translation (New York: McGraw-Hill Book Company, 1964), 60 vols.; Vol. 6, *The Trinity*, trans. Ceslaus Velecky, I, 30, 4, c: "For names of genera or species (for instance 'animal' or 'man' [*homo*]) are used to refer to the common natures themselves, not to the logical status of such natures, to which terms like 'genus' or 'species' refer."

14. See Aristotle, *Topics*, I, 5–9. In a short work attributed to Thomas Aquinas, "On the Nature of Accidents" (*De Natura Accidentorum*, Opusculum 38 in Vol. 15 of the Parma Edition [P. Fiaccadori, 1852–73] of his *Opera Omnia*), the following explanation is given: "It must be understood therefore that 'accident' has two meanings, a natural and a logical; naturally, as accident is distinguished from substance, and this includes the nine genera of accidents; but logically, accident is said to be one of the five universals of which Porphyry speaks. Therefore accident understood in the first way follows the nature of the thing, and accident understood in the second way follows the operation of the intellect, which makes universality in things...." (my translation). Mortimer Adler considered the question of the nature and status of the predicables in *Problems for Thomists: The Problem of Species* (New York: Sheed & Ward, 1940).

15. In Peter Hoeg's novel, *Smilla's Sense of Snow*, (New York: Dell Publishing Company, 1993) the action hinges upon the knowledge of these different kinds of snow.

16. A physical basis for categorizing is being studied: "... in the last decade researchers have tentatively identified roughly 20 categories that the brain seems to use to organize knowledge. Among them are fruits and vegetables, plants, animals, body parts, colors, numbers, letters, nouns, verbs, proper names, faces, facial expressions, several different emotions and several different features of sound. '... it seems

clearer and clearer the knowledge is organized in bits distributed widely across the cortex.'"—Dr. Nina Dronkers, quoted in Philip J. Hilts, "Brain's Memory System Comes into Focus," *The New York Times*, 30 May 1995, 6(B).

17. See Aristotle *Physics* (hereafter: *Phys.*) 1.1.184a18. Submicroscopic entities can help to explain the way things appear at the level of ordinary human observation, but the investigation begins at the human level.

18. Aristotle *Phys.* 1.2.184b27–185b1; and *Met.* (Z) 7.3.1029a30–33; 7.1032a15–20; 16.1040b18–25.

19. P. F. Strawson, in *Individuals: An Essay in Descriptive Metaphysics* (Garden City, NY: Doubleday & Company, 1963) argues to the conclusion that *person* is the primitive concept by comparison with Descartes's *mind* and *body*.

20. See Heribert Mühlen, *L'Esprit dans l'Eglise*, trans. A. Liefooghe, M. Mussart and R. Virrion (Paris: Les Editions du Cerf, 1969), 44, citing M. Schmaus, *Katholische Dogmatik* (Munich: M. Hueber, 1956), III, II, 51: "One must by necessity of principle say with M. Schmaus, that 'the categories elaborated by Aristotle correspond to the being of nature, but not to the being of the person.'"

2

Dewey's Dissatisfaction

*[P]ersonality is the one thing of permanent and abiding worth, and ... in
every human individual there lies personality.*

—John Dewey

PERSON AS AGENT

John Dewey is one of the few philosophical writers to consider how the word
'person' is applied in various disciplines. In some seventy years of writing books,
essays, forewords, and book reviews he established himself as one of the most
influential American philosophers of his day. He was particularly interested in
educational and political philosophy, and the notion of the person serves as the
organizing principle of his work in these areas.

While he did at times use the word 'person' in different ways, Dewey found
the most fundamental meaning of the word to be that of the person as a legal
entity. In a letter Dewey says that

> certain business men are insurance *agents* and others are *agents* with respect
> to other humans who are "principals." What I want to do is in effect to
> interpret the words "self," "person," etc., in terms analogous to the social-
> behavioral use of "agent" in such cases as I've mentioned.[1]

It is this emphasis upon agency that characterizes Dewey's treatment of the
human persons on many different occasions throughout his philosophical
career.

FROM SOUL TO HABIT AND SITUATION

As the psychologist Gordon Allport, himself an astute student of personality,
points out in his article on "Dewey's Individual and Social Psychology,"[2] Dewey's
thought evolved over the course of time, from a use of 'soul' to undergird
psychological capacities, to a resolute renunciation of soul or subject in favor
of habit and situation.[3] Certain tendencies dominate his treatment of the no-

18

tion of person, however, and these become clearer toward the end of his life. Dewey notes in his long article on corporate personality that

Just as the law has grown by taking unto itself *practices* of antecedent non-legal status, so it has grown by taking . . . from psychology or philosophy or whatnot extraneous *dogmas* and *ideas*.[4]

Dewey's intention to clear up the confusion in the language of the law fit in well with his conception of logic as a discipline of inquiry rather than as a means of setting forth static truths. Elsewhere he points to what he perceives as a weakness of the old logic:

The discussion goes on in terms of *the* state, *the* individual; the nature of institutions as such, society in general. . . . Hence they do not assist inquiry. They close it. . . . we want to know about *some* state.[5]

In 1902–03, he offered a detailed critique of Royce's view of person as it related to self and consciousness. And in his *Cyclopedia* article of 1912–14, he contrasted person and individual, as well as the ancient Roman conception of person and that of Kant. In that article he says, "Personality expresses what one *has*—a property that one may acquire. . . ."[6]

Although some facets of Dewey's thought did change over his lifetime, his taste for the concrete and practical was constant and enduring. He felt strongly—perhaps in reaction to his early Hegelian studies—that it was useless, even harmful, to formulate purely theoretical doctrines of the person. In 1942 he cited Hitler as an example of someone who speaks about personality with malevolent intent:

idealism and personality separated from empirical analysis and experimental utilization of concrete social situations are worse than vague mouthings. They stand for "realities" . . . that are the plans and desires of those who wish to gain control. . . .[7]

Dewey's lifelong interest in the nature of human personality is apparent: he wrote a definition of person for an encyclopedia. He reproached Hitler for speaking of persons in a laudatory fashion while in practice attacking their rights. The person as a freely functioning individual human being in a democratic society was an ideal for him. Yet when Allport, speaking as a friendly critic, found Dewey's account of the person inadequate, Dewey had no satisfactory reply to the criticism. Thus, despite all his work on the human person, Dewey had no finished notion of the person even late in his philosophical career.

POSSIBLE REASONS FOR DEWEY'S DISSATISFACTION

An explanation for this lack of success of Dewey's endeavors may lie in his decision to trace the word 'person' to its Latin source alone. The Latin source is, of course, heavily influenced by Roman law, where the person is seen essentially as a being in context, as enabled by and embedded in the legal structure.

What he chose to ignore was the development of a somewhat different Greek tradition stemming from the understanding of the person as a substantial being, existent in the physical world, thinkable apart from his legal status. However, this was not just a casual oversight.

Dewey more than once mentions pejoratively the "Hellenic-medieval" tradition.[8] In particular, he sought to substitute for an Aristotelian logic of timeless forms of knowledge, a logic of inquiry better fitted to the reality of modern scientific method.[9]

Dewey saw the ancient philosophy as an attempt to get at Reality, whereas the new logic he advocated would question nature and thus discover new truths. Dewey thinks that Aristotle lacked this logic of discovery.

> Metaphysics is a substitute for custom as the source and guarantor of higher moral and social values—that is the leading theme of the classic philosophy of Europe, as evolved by Plato and Aristotle—a philosophy, let us always recall, renewed and restated by the Christian philosophy of Medieval Europe.[10]

The present inquiry attempts to show, in the light of logical considerations, that Dewey's theory is ultimately incoherent because of this critical oversight. In addition, I hope to discover what would be needed to make his theory—or a theory like it—more adequate. In what follows I offer a detailed analysis of Dewey's observations as found in his published works.[11]

PERSONALITY IN THE EARLY WORKS

Dewey's first statement of his position regarding the human person as a political being appears in an essay, in 1888, occasioned by Sir Henry Maine's book, *Popular Government*:

> ordinary objections to democracy rest upon ideas which conceive of it after the type of an individualism of a numerical character; and [I] have tried to suggest that democracy is an ethical idea, the idea of a personality, with truly infinite capacities, incorporate with every man.[12]

The ancient Greek civilization in which Plato and Aristotle flourished took for granted the necessity of slavery. Members of a certain class of human beings were destined to do the work needed to provide the material means of life for a more privileged citizen class. Members of the citizen class were seen as the only ones capable of living an ethical life in ancient Athens. Dewey identifies the practice of slavery as the weakness of ancient society; and he finds the source of this error in a division of human life into "two parts, one animal, the other truly human and therefore truly ethical."[13] He, on the other hand, insists that every person, even in his work life, enters into the ethical life of his society. And further that "all industrial relations are to be regarded as subordinate to human relations, to the law of personality."[14]

Personality guarantees equality since it is found among all human beings. Also it is in society that a human individual learns what personality means, although "personality cannot be procured for any one. . . ."[15] Dewey says further that in a democracy, liberty "is the ethical idea that personality is the supreme and only law, that every man is an absolute end in himself."[16]

Ten years later, Dewey again found an opportunity to air his views about personality when he reviewed James Mark Baldwin's *Social and Ethical Interpretations in Mental Development: A Study in Social Psychology*. Baldwin saw imitation as fundamental in personality development, but did not explain how what is distinctively individual in the person can emerge in society. Dewey severely criticized him for vagueness and inconsistency in failing to make clear how the individual person can be said to be social. Does society, Dewey wondered, make the individual social, or is there a "common content" in the minds of individuals that makes them effectively social?[17]

PERSON IN THE MIDDLE WORKS

Early in the new century, Dewey published a paper in which he makes clear that his interest in the person was not merely theoretical, as might have been supposed from his criticism of Baldwin. In this work he shows how he conceives personality in relation to "mechanisms" like attention and emotion that function, so to speak, within persons. Teachers must not regard the child simply as an "unanalyzed personality,"[18] but must take into account the various factors that enter into the formation of the child's behavior.

> Teachers will tell you that a child is careless or inattentive. . . . Now it is only through some recognition of attention as a mechanism, some awareness of the interplay of sensations, images and motor impulses which constitute it as an objective fact that the teacher can deal effectively with attention as a function.[19]

In a striking phrase, he continues:

> The ethical personality does not go to school naked; it takes with it the body as the instrument through which all influences reach it, and through control of which its ideas are both elaborated and expressed. The teacher does not deal with personality at large, but as expressed in intellectual and practical impulses and habits.[20]

Dewey's characteristic practical, concrete, analytical approach to the question of the human person is evident in these passages. He is always suspicious of theories that have no correlate in experience. In 1902 he reviewed Josiah Royce's *Gifford Lectures, Nature, Man, and the Moral Order*. Royce proposed a view of the person based on the notion of time rates of mental processes.[21] Dewey is quite impatient with Royce's formulation, declaring that "this whole doctrine of 'nature' is too high for me;" and that it tends to bring philosophy into disrepute.

An article appearing in 1907 on the topic, "Does Reality Possess Practical Characteristics?" brings to light another of Dewey's lifelong themes: the centrality of the person in all aspects of life. He questions why the philosophy of the time tends to use the expression "merely personal" for everything of a practical nature.

> What becomes of philosophy so far as humane and liberal interests are concerned, if, in an age when the person and the personal loom large in politics, industry, religion, art, and science, it contents itself with this parrot cry of phenomenalism, whenever the personal comes into view?[22]

Dewey's article on "Personality" in the *Cyclopedia of Education* (1912–13) enabled him to summarize his views on the person. He treats the topic in relation to 'self' and 'individual', beginning with the concept of person as it developed in connection with Roman law. According to that law, slaves were not persons, nor were minors, except through others. Dewey notes that as "the external traits of this legal view disappeared, an ethical sense developed out of them, . . ." a sense, Dewey says, that Kant later formulated in his law that "A person is an end in and for himself, never a means to anything beyond."[23] Here again, Dewey confines his observations to the ancient Roman legal and the modern moral theories, without devoting any attention to a physical or metaphysical theory of the sort that he sometimes refers to as the "Hellenic-medieval."

Dewey also contrasts 'person' and 'individual' in this article. Personality, he thinks, is often regarded as a "higher" idea than individuality. But again, true to his preference for the concrete, he does not find the abstraction of personality so helpful as the contrasting notion of individuality. "All persons have personality in the same sense," Dewey says. But individuality is deeper because it "is always differential" and "expresses what one uniquely *is*," rather than what one *has*. He adds that in a democratic era, children, once seen by law as like slaves, except that the child was potentially a person, have had "rights of personality" extended to them, with an impact upon educational methods. He concludes that "No consistent theory upon this point has, however, as yet, been worked out in practice."[24]

In his *Reconstruction in Philosophy* (1920), Dewey reviewed the history of the development of modern society out of the medieval, making the observation that "The greatest influence of Protestantism was . . . in developing the idea of the personality of every human being as an end in himself."[25] This took place, Dewey thinks, because individual human beings began to see themselves as in a direct relationship with God, not needing the mediation of the church. He remarks also that each person must have a responsible share in shaping the policies of groups to which he belongs.

It was in this work that Dewey pointed out as a weakness of the old logic its search for generality. He remarks that the old logic reflects a "pre-scientific state of human affairs, concerns, interests, and ends," and it is not adequate because we do not have ready-made categories to deal with new problems.[26]

LATER WORKS: CORPORATE PERSONALITY

Dewey's longest discussion of the subject of personality is in the article entitled "Corporate Personality" published in 1926 in the *Yale Law Journal.* He puts his point briefly: "'person' signifies what law makes it signify."[27] In justifying his own venture into the field of law he echoes an earlier statement:

> discussions and theories which have influenced legal practice have, with respect to the concept of 'person,' introduced and depended upon a mass of non-legal considerations: considerations popular, historical, political, moral, philosophical, metaphysical and, in connection with the latter, theological.[28]

Dewey begins his discussion by citing definitions of person as a "subject of rights-duties," cautioning his reader, however, against looking for a genus of "subject," which has no more genus than "dry" in wine and in things lacking moisture.[29] Authors who look for a common genus for the legal and the "natural" (i.e., philosophical, psychological, etc.) person perpetuate, he thinks, a similar confusion. What is needed, instead, is to "overhaul" the doctrine of personality. Even for those who find *will* to be involved in the notion of personality, the need to define 'will' involves recourse to the same logical question: Is definition a matter of finding an essential inhering nature or of discovering consequences and relations?[30]

If the definition of a legal subject, then, is a "matter of analysis of facts, not of search for an inhering essence," still the consequences in terms of which the analysis will be carried on "must be social in character, and . . . controlled and modified by being the bearing of rights and obligations. . . ."[31] Dewey concludes the first part of his article with the statement that:

> Neglect may . . . be made into a positive and intrinsic force or agency by hypostatization, but this is parallel to the procedure of school-teachers who make a positive existential entity out of "inattention."[32]

Dewey sums up the discussion so far with a clear statement of its purpose:

> to show the logical method by which . . . a definition [of person] should be arrived at; and, secondly, to show that the question has been enormously complicated by the employment of a wrong logical method, and by the

introduction of irrelevant conceptions, imported into legal discussion . . . from uncritical popular beliefs, from psychology, and from a metaphysics ultimately derived from theology.[33]

The second part of the article is devoted to a historical survey of some of the factors influencing the development of this notion in ancient and medieval times. He cites

the definition of St. Thomas Aquinas, *vera persona est rei rationabilis individua substantia*. In this definition every one of the three last words has a technical meaning that goes back to the metaphysical discussions of Aristotle; the problem of the nature of the "individual" being, indeed, for Middle Age philosophers, even more of a problem than that of "substance."[34]

He adds in a note:

We are far away from the Latin *persona* which when applied to a man in the concrete hardly meant more than a separate physical body. The change in meaning was undoubtedly of theological origin, the term "*persona*" having been applied by the fathers (first I believe by Tertullian) to the hypostases of the Trinity.[35]

It is clear to Dewey that this

conception of "person" endured long after the metaphysics and theology which gave it birth were obscured if not forgotten; and they account for much of the difficulty in even recent discussions in attributing "person" to corporate as well as to single units.[36]

In the eighteenth and nineteenth centuries, Dewey finds a change in the

concept of the "singular person," now become the full-fledged individual in his own right. . . . the single person, as the "real person," is no longer either a physical body or a rational substance. These two meanings persist, but they are covered up with vestments derived from the theory of natural rights inhering in individual persons as such.[37]

In the third part of his article, Dewey sums up the findings of his survey:

The fact of the case is that there is no clear-cut unity, logical or practical, throughout the different theories which have been advanced and which are still advanced in behalf of the "real" personality of either "natural" or associated persons.[38]

The outcome of his discussion of the history of the notion of corporate personality is "to enforce the value of eliminating the *idea* of personality until the concrete facts and relations involved here have been faced and stated on their own account."[39]

This brief survey of Dewey's article, while not exhausting its contents, especially those of a technical legal sort, does make clear that he was not much interested in using technical philosophical terms like 'hypostasis'[40] and 'substance' to speak about the person; that he found the Aristotelian logic of proof inadequate to the scientific logic needed today (he does not advert to the logic of discovery Aristotle talks about in *Posterior Analytics*);[41] and that he saw no point in pursuing a quest for a genus of 'person', natural and social. At the same time he situates the notion of person directly in the social sphere.

In an article written about the same time as Dewey's "Corporate Personality," he discusses Locke's ideas of substance and relation, both, somewhat curiously, in reference to the *predicable* accident, with no reference to the *predicamental* meaning of either substance or relation (i.e., "something able to *be in itself*," and "that which *exists in reference to another*.")[42] He treats substance as that which possesses the generic and specific qualities that define an essence, and accident as what does not enter into the definition, nor follow necessarily from the essence. But Dewey does not give these distinctions and explanations of predicamental and predicable accidents; one is left to wonder whether he in fact confused the two.[43] The point is somewhat subtle. Let us once again consider the distinction between them.

Predicamental accident is simply a word or phrase, one of nine, definable as a fundamental way of being or being said: "in reference to another," in the example just given. (See Chapter 1). *Predicable* accident, on the other hand, is the name given to the logical relation between a predicate and a subject in a sentence: it is so called because it is related, as predicate to a subject, in a way that is merely accidental. Let us consider an example: Kevin is red-headed in real life. When I talk about his being so, I am treating his red-headedness under the title of the category of quality. I may also think of it, however, as a *predicable* accident, so called because of its "accidental" *relationship* to the subject, Kevin, in this sentence: "Kevin is red-headed." Here the quality, "red-headed," is called "accidental" because it could change, for example, to grey, in reality. By contrast, "*risible*" (being able to laugh) is the example usually given of a (predicable) *property* of a human being, something harder to change than hair color. Although properties do not belong to the essence of human nature, they are said to be consequent upon being a human being.

Dewey gives no indication of being aware of the difference when he thus defines (predicable) accident: "The meaning of 'accident' is determined by contrast with *essence*. That which is accidental is no part of essence and does not follow in any way from essence."[44] Whereas predicable accidents are logical relations called "accidents" because of their nonessential *relation* to the subject of the sentence, predicamental accidents—also called categories—can refer to real modifications of the substance itself, relation being one of nine possible modifications. In a sense, then, to speak of "relation" as a predicable accident is to see it as twice related. In any case, given Dewey's commitment to a logic of discovery rather than to what he saw as the static logic of ancient Greece and the Middle Ages, it is likely that these considerations meant little to him.

In 1931 Dewey reviewed F. Hallis's *Corporate Personality: A Study in Jurisprudence*. Dewey observes that Hallis "holds that it is necessary to maintain that the legal concept of personality really has something in common with the philosophical concept in its non-legal sense."[45] Dewey finds Hallis's solutions ultimately unsatisfactory. To him they seem to be "hardly more than verbal assertions that both the rational and the empirical factors [accounting for individual personality as well as social groups] *must* be united in a valid theory."[46] Perhaps Hallis might have responded that Dewey merely makes "verbal assertions" of his own point of view.

For Dewey, the person performs some of his highest functions as citizen, and there is a reciprocal enhancement of individual and society. In his 1937 article entitled "All Life Educative," Dewey states emphatically what he sees to be the ultimate objective of a democratic society: "For only as all institutions and relations contribute to development of personality in a cooperative society is democracy effective."[47]

In a new edition (1939) of his *Freedom and Culture* (originally published in 1915), Dewey vigorously attacked Hitler's use of the word 'personality', showing it to be too abstract, "without regard to concrete social context, and, indeed, as if the bare principle of a personal self automatically produced its own proper social context."[48] Hitler contrasted the "principle of democracy . . . and the principle of personality, which is the principle of achievement."[49] Dewey continues his vigorous denunciation of the Nazi tyranny:

> The authority which Hitler gives to personality is that of active or vital energy; . . . But the passages should make clear the emptiness of formal philosophical and theological assertion of the supreme value of "personality," exactly as other utterances make evident the barrenness . . . of idealism.[50]

Dewey here points to an important principle in validating any theory of person: its empirical working out in practice. Dewey himself could be accused, however, of failing to offer a theory of personality that could stand up to criticism by someone who wished to make society, any society, the source of the dignity and rights of the person.

CONCLUSION: AN ADEQUATE NATURALISM

Dewey often described his position as "naturalism." It is interesting to speculate upon whether he might have found Aristotle's natural philosophy and inductive logic more congenial than he did if he had known them better. Annette Baier, in her Presidential Address[51] delivered before the Eastern Division of the American Philosophical Association in 1990, remarked on the "schizophrenia of modern philosophy of mind and of the person," and also observed that "a naturalist will keep in view the full range of what we claim as our own."[52] Dewey's account of the person would perhaps have been more satisfactory if it had been closer to Baier's (whose "full range" includes religious realities as well as realities of other sorts) instead of excluding what he saw as unproductive lines of thought in explaining reality.

Dewey is probably as close to a "philosopher laureate" as the United States has ever come. His theory of personality is in many ways illuminating, and his insistence on a naturalist approach to the study of the person is welcome. Yet it was ultimately unsatisfactory even to him, particularly in its endeavor to make the person central to the various sciences. It may be worthwhile then to investigate the line of thought he consciously avoided, the "Hellenic-medieval" doctrines he found too static. This will be the object of Part 2 of the present work, in which the sources of the word 'person' and of the various philosophical terms used to elucidate it will be considered.

NOTES

1. Darnell Rucker, "Selves Into Persons: Another Legacy from John Dewey," in Konstantin Kolenda, ed., *Person and Community in American Philosophy*, Rice University Studies, 66, no. 4 (fall 1980): 107. Rucker considers unpublished works of Dewey, especially an article, "Persons and Things." I am concentrating on Dewey's published works, and not on every one of them, but quite narrowly upon those in which he formally introduces the notion of person. For a more complete and rounded view of his notion of person as it functions in his philosophy as a whole, see his *Reconstruction in Philosophy* (Boston: Beacon Press, 1948), 193–198; *Individualism Old and New* (New York: Minton, Balch & Company, 1930), 166–69; and *Experience and Nature* (New York: W. W. Norton & Company, 1929), Chap. VI, for example. See also Robert J. Roth, *John Dewey and Self-Realization* (Englewood Cliffs, NJ: Prentice-Hall, 1963) and Robert Westbrook, *John Dewey and American Democracy* (Ithaca: Cornell University Press, 1991).
2. Paul Arthur Schilpp, ed., *The Philosophy of John Dewey* (New York: Tudor Publishing Company, 1939), 276, 555. For Allport's own study of the meaning of personhood, see his *Personality: A Psychological Interpretation* (New York: Henry Holt and Company, 1937), especially Chapter 2.
3. Schilpp, *Dewey*, 267; see "Doctor Martineau's Theory of Morals," in *The Collected Works of John Dewey*, JoAnn Boydston, ed., (Carbondale: Southern Illinois University Press, 1969), The Later Works, 17, 1–6. References to Dewey's collected works will be given hereafter in the form: EW for Early Works, MW for Middle Works, and LW for Later Works of Dewey, with volume and page number.
4. Dewey, "Corporate Personality," *The Collected Works of John Dewey*, JoAnn Boydston, ed., (Carbondale: Southern Illinois University Press, 1969), The Later Works, 2, 25. He continues: "We often go on discussing problems in terms of old ideas when the solution of the problem depends upon getting rid of the old ideas, and putting in their place concepts more in accord with the present state of ideas and knowledge."

   And: "'Subject' and 'subjectivity' occupy in modern German philosophy . . . the place taken in ancient metaphysics by 'substance' and also by 'subject' of a judgment in a logical sense," (ibid., 27). Again, "The Greek urn as well as the Greek statue and temple were works of art. . . . Such objects, or subjects, are *substances* having design and form in an objective sense."—*Logic: The Theory of Inquiry*, 5 (LW 12, 89).

5. Dewey, "Reconstruction as Affecting Social Philosophy," in *Reconstruction in Philosophy*, MW 12, 188, Chap. 8, 187–201.

6. Dewey, "Personality," in *Cyclopedia of Education*, MW 7, 296.

7. Dewey, "The One-World of Hitler's National Socialism," MW 8, 432.

8. Dewey, "Freedom and Culture," LW 13, 148.

9. Dewey, "Significance of Logical Reconstruction," MW 12, 189.

10. Dewey, "The Needed Reform of Logic," MW 12, 89.

11. See Rucker, op. cit., 112: "Previous theory, Dewey points out, inverted the actual order of relations, holding that moral relations exist because humans are intrinsically persons; whereas what actually occurs is that humans *become* persons with the rise of offices having moral qualities."

12. Dewey, "The Ethics of Democracy," 227–49, EW 1, 248.

13. Ibid., EW 1, 247.

14. Ibid.

15. Ibid., EW 1, 244–46.

16. Ibid., EW 1, 245.

17. "(not being sufficiently familiar with Aristotle and Hegel), I confess I should have thought that the chief value of the genetic method was that it enabled us to *substitute* a scientific statement of the nature of personality and society, and their relations to each other, for a metaphysical one." Dewey, "Rejoinder to Baldwin's Reply," EW 5, 400.

18. Dewey, "Psychology and Social Practice," MW 1, 138.

19. Ibid., 139.

20. Ibid., MW 1, 139.

21. MW 2, 127, n. 2. For Royce, "the 'person' is that the time rate of whose mental process is sufficiently like our own to enter into direct communication with it; the 'thing' belongs to some consciousness whose time rate is disparate from our own." See Part 3, Chapter 12, below, for a discussion of the importance of time for the person.

22. Dewey, "Does Reality Possess Practical Characteristics?" MW 4, 126.

23. Dewey, "Personality," MW 7, 295.

24. Ibid., MW 7, 296.

25. John Dewey, *Reconstruction in Philosophy*, MW 12, 105. See also Jean-Marc Chappuis, "The Reformation and the Formation of the Person," *The Ecumenical Review*, 39, no. 1 (January 1987) 4ff., for a detailed explanation of this position, although with no reference to Dewey. "Through the vicissitudes of history, this Christian personalism was to bear fruit in Calvinism as it had earlier done in the Benedictine tradition and, indeed, with the same characteristics: the study of holy scripture, meditation, psychological introspection, the interiorization of the personal conscience, a certain alienation or detachment from the world together with an active acceptance of responsibility for the world, profound inner conviction being the mainspring of action" (6).

26. Dewey, *Reconstruction*, MW 12, Chap. VIII. See also the new Introduction to the 1948 edition, III, xxvii.

27. Dewey, "Corporate Personality," LW 2, 22.

28. Ibid., LW 2, 22. For some of the influences shaping Dewey's religious attitudes, see Robert B. Westbrook, op. cit., 30–31, 35–36, and 79.

29. Ibid., LW 2, 23.
30. Ibid., LW 2, 25, 28–9. Dewey refers to the logicians C. S. Peirce and A. N. Whitehead.
31. Ibid., LW 2, 29.
32. Ibid., LW 2, 31; cf. Dewey, "Psychology and Practice," MW 1, 139.
33. Dewey, "Corporate Personality," LW 2, 31-32.
34. Ibid., 34.
35. Ibid.
36. Ibid., 34–35.
37. Ibid., 37.
38. Ibid., LW 2, 38.
39. Ibid., LW 2, 43.
40. Cf. Dewey, *The Logic of Inquiry*, LW 12, 516.
41. See Aristotle *Posterior Analytics* 1.2.71b8–17; 18.81a37–81b9; 2.19.99b15–100b17. A. Gratry's *Logic*, trans. Helen Singer and Milton Singer (La Salle, Il.: The Open Court Publishing Company, 1944), which was praised by the Booles and C. S. Peirce in the last century, discusses the use of reasoning called "induction" in detail from a historical point of view. Gratry also produced an original theory of human nature and the person based upon classical sources and St. Augustine, in which he emphasized the "root" of the soul, seen as a power underlying intellect and will—Augustine's "memory" understood as consciousness.
42. Dewey, "Substance, Power and Quality in Locke," LW 2, 147.
43. Did Dewey see the categories and predicables of Aristotle through Kantian lenses? Intending to set forth that "In every judgment there is a concept which holds of many representations, and among them of a given representation that is immediately related to an object," Kant seeks the unity to be found in every judgment, thus finding under the heading of "relation" the (Kantian) category of "substance." See Immanuel Kant, *Critique of Pure Reason*, trans. Norman Kemp Smith (New York: St. Martin's Press, 1965), B93–106.
44. Dewey, *Logic: The Theory of Inquiry*, LW 12, 94.
45. Dewey, LW 6, 268.
46. Ibid., LW 6, 270.
47. Dewey, "All Life Educative," LW 11, 539.
48. Dewey, "Freedom and Culture," MW 8, 431.
49. Ibid., MW 8, 431–32.
50. Ibid., MW 8, 432.
51. Annette Baier, "A Naturalist View of Persons," American Philosophical Association, *Proceedings and Addresses*, 65, 3 (November 1991), 5–17.
52. Annette Baier, op. cit., 12, 10. Robert J. Roth, *John Dewey and Self-Realization* (Englewood Cliffs, NJ: Prentice Hall, Inc., 1962), explains the relation between Dewey's naturalism, which sees human beings as at one with the natural world, and his objections to any intrusion from a "supernatural" religion or a transcendent God. See Chap. VI, 100–126.

3

Marcel's Philosophy of the Person

How can we resist the temptation to hypostatize the person...?

—Gabriel Marcel

CENTRALITY OF PERSON FOR MARCEL

Like Dewey, Gabriel Marcel made the person central to his philosophy. Born into a distinguished family, Marcel experienced a lonely childhood in which imaginary companions played a consoling part. Perhaps as a result, the person as a related being became central to his drama as well as to his phenomenological philosophy. Marcel sees the person as called to respond in faithful love and hope to the others in the midst of whom he finds himself situated. Having achieved the degree of *Agregé* in philosophy at the Sorbonne, he pursued his own distinctive style of philosophizing. It could perhaps be characterized as pushing the limits of the given, the objectified and the problematic.[1]

Some of the features of Marcel's philosophy most relevant to the central idea of the person will be singled out here for comment, particularly the notions of responsibility, confrontation, being in a situation, mystery, and freedom. Marcel, who is often called an Existentialist, sees the person as *homo viator*, the human being on a journey, called to rebuild a shattered world, obliged to "cut himself a dangerous path across the unsteady blocks of a universe which has collapsed."[2]

MARCEL AGAINST FICHTE

Early in his philosophical work, Marcel became exasperated with the Fichtean deduction of the empirical self from the transcendental self, urging that "what exists... is... an individual, the real individual that I am, with the unbelievably minute details of my experience."[3] This early reaction against the "impersonal or the immanent"[4] later became concentrated in an interest in the person as revelatory of being.

At the beginning of the second part of his *Metaphysical Journal,* Marcel inscribed this passage from E. M. Forster's novel, *Howard's End:* "It is private life that holds out the mirror to infinity; personal intercourse, and that alone, that ever hints at a personality beyond our daily vision."

Later he pointed out that Forster's thought here embodies two of the central preoccupations of his own career as a thinker: the concern (*exigence*) for *being* and for *beings.*[5] These concerns may seem contradictory at first, but while it is true that Marcel's plays are predominantly focused upon persons—beings— and his philosophy upon being, Marcel the philosopher remains close to the concrete data of the situation from which he draws his conclusions.

ACT AND CONFRONTATION

This early interest in the concrete helps to explain why Marcel, in his later formal treatment, considers the person in light of that person's acts, characteristically proposing to re-examine "those ideas which lie ready to hand and considering them from the start in terms of their rootedness in personal experience."[6]

'Act', he points out, is opposed in common speech to 'velleity', to 'mere words'. Velleity suggests powerlessness, a fearful, divided, hesitant state. The word that is a mere word does not subsist, is not effective, "passes over reality like a wind." But "act" is essentially that which can change a situation. Not every change, however, results from an act. A "gesture" (*geste*), for example a theft by a kleptomaniac, brings about a change, but only in a rather accidental fashion.

What, then, distinguishes an act in the full sense of the term from a gesture? In the first place, the "act . . . has certain contours. . . . We have to be able to reply *yes* or *no* to any question relating to it." One who has nursed a difficult invalid until his death might find it impossible to answer a clear yes or no to the question, "Did you desire the death of this invalid?" To the extent that he is unable to answer this question, his deed is less an act.[7]

Furthermore, "The reality of the act is by no means exhausted in the apparent accomplishment of a task." Rather, it is of "the essence of the act to *commit* the agent."[8] Just what is this commitment?

> what is characteristic of my act is that it can later be claimed (*revendiqué*) by me; it is basically as though I signed in advance an admission: the day on which I shall be faced with my act, whether by others or by myself, . . . I should be able to say: yes, it is indeed I who have acted thus, *ego sum qui feci.*[9]

To shirk later would be to deny oneself, to introduce into oneself a duality "destructive of my own reality."[10] Marcel thinks an act must involve responsibility: "In other words, there is no act without responsibility." To refuse to assume responsibility for my acts is to "annul myself as subject, as person."[11]

Somehow a person's act becomes part of one. And as an act it is good or evil. The more it approaches indifference, the less does it partake of the nature of an act.

Because it is something so personal, 'act' cannot strictly be defined. It always implies reference to a person, and to a person as such—not to my hand, as I write this, but to me, the person writing. "An act is all the more act, I should say, as it is less possible for me to repudiate it without completely denying myself."[12]

The notion of person becomes clear in reference to the preceding discussion of act when a person is contrasted with the *on* (one, as in "one thinks"). The impersonal *on* or "they" is by definition anonymous, faceless; it eludes me, it is essentially irresponsible, and "in a certain sense the very contrary of agent."[13] To the extent that a person's opinions are indistinguishable from those of his newspaper, he is penetrated by the impersonal "they," the locus of flight and evasion, whereas the property of the person is "to face, to confront," (*affronter*).[14] The person's characteristic virtue is courage, courage to take responsibility; and by his courageous confronting of the *on*, he shatters it.

Marcel explains that "*confronting*" involves a kind of envisioning of a situation. To envisage a situation in its tangled actuality is to evaluate it, for it forces a person to calculate chances, to appraise it, since "a situation is in its very essence, something which is not altogether clear; . . ."[15] In a very dense passage, Marcel develops the related notions of envisaging, evaluating, appraising, and confronting the situation. "For to confront is to expose myself, i.e., to orient myself in a certain way, in a determinate direction, and only an appraisal can fix this direction."[16]

To clarify his meaning, Marcel here introduces the example of a person who goes against the current of opinion as represented by the newspapers, basing his stand on his intimate knowledge of the situation, and in so doing exposes himself and assumes responsibility for his stand. By thus taking responsibility for his acts, the person is somehow "joined to himself." Neighbors who suspect serious child abuse is occurring but take no action to stop it would no doubt be seen by Marcel as lacking in the civic and personal responsibility proper to persons.

Finally, "to assume is in a sense to confront, but curiously enough, to confront one's own past: i.e., something which is already behind one."[17] Just as confronting a person's own past is taking responsibility for it, so confronting a situation is in a sense accepting it as one's own.[18]

Marcel refuses to identify the person with the individual. The individual for Marcel is the *on* in a parcelled-out state. Thus to define the individual is by no means to define the person; in fact such a definition should not be attempted, as it is ultimately inappropriate to the person.

I believe, on the one hand, that the person is not and cannot be an essence, and on the other hand, that any metaphysics . . . somehow established apart from, or protected from essences, is in danger of collapsing like a house of cards.[19]

In Marcel's view, the person is neither a variety nor an enhancement (*promotion*) of the individual: "there is absolutely no sense whatever in asking oneself in the presence of a given being: is this or is this not a person?" Nor can we say universally that every individual rises to the level of the person: "we can neither grant that this promotion is universal, nor that it is not."[20]

We must grant, however, that just as the person in confronting the *on* tends to reduce it (by asking, for instance, "Who says?" when it is alleged that "They say . . ."), so the person confronting the individual tends to make of the individual a person, and it is in this way that justice is possible, through this "irradiation" of the person, so that justice is as characteristic of the person as courage or sincerity.[21]

Metaphysics Inadequate

This much granted, however, Marcel refuses to draw any metaphysical conclusions as to the essence of the person:

as soon as we try to express all of this in metaphysical terms, . . . we encounter serious difficulties. . . . How can we resist the temptation to hypostatize the person, question oneself about the nature of this principle which confronts, evaluates, assumes?
. . . we cannot in fact treat the person either as a datum, or perhaps even as an existent. At bottom, our formula: *the characteristic of the person is to confront*, reveals its inadequacy in so far as it cuts off, at least implicitly, the person from the act in which the former realizes himself. . . . every theory of the person is in danger of somehow exploiting this unwarranted cleavage.[22]

Marcel is convinced that any theory that would introduce the idea of a division between person and act cannot be sustained. Even to think of the person as a "connecting link" between successive acts would be to take too theoretical a view of act and person, looking at the act from outside. But act, as act, is personal, not open to inspection from without.

The question can only be asked when we shift to another meaning and the act is envisaged as an operation; for wherever there is an operation we are naturally entitled to ask who the operator is. This shifting over is in fact altogether inevitable: . . . we are individuals, we are exposed on all sides to the impersonal *one*; . . .[23]

To push the metaphysical analysis of person farther would result in seeing act and person from the point of view of a *spectator*. This results in constructing a synthetic unity, an "entity endowed with a certain number of abstract characteristics."[24]

In what is perhaps intended as a play on the Latin meaning of *persona*, as a mask worn by an actor, Marcel concludes that perhaps

> the person can become a reality only in God. For the rest of us, the person is perhaps but a point of view . . . always in danger of degenerating into an attitude or into a palpitating anticipation, an appearance which can be degraded at any moment, can harden into disguise, or can by some unholy masquerade, become a parody of itself.[25]

Or, on the other hand, perhaps the

> person is correlative with that anonymous or disguised factor which it confronts to the very end, and . . . in God, in whom this factor disappears, the person is abolished, simply because it is here that it fully emerges into the light.
>   It would be worthwhile to examine closely these two alternatives and to ask whether the opposition here between the two is not more verbal than real.[26]

Perhaps it is impossible to carry the metaphysical analysis of person further. The consequences of this notion for other parts of Marcel's philosophy, however, can be seen in both his dramatic and his philosophical works. He emphasizes that there is a "bond between my philosophical thought and my dramatic work."[27] In the plays he shows human beings in the act of realizing or failing to realize themselves as true human persons. Marcel appears to derive many of his philosophical insights from a consideration of the acts of the characters in his own plays. Here his more strictly philosophical statements will be considered.

First of all, the person alone, Marcel says, is educable. The anonymous, faceless masses can indeed be trained, but they are by definition incapable of the *acts* of intelligence through which education is possible.[28] In a prescient insight into the effects of television upon the undiscriminating crowd, he says that passive viewers accept their opinions ready-made from the media of mass communication without having had to put forth the effort necessary to create these instruments of communication. These viewers thus become victims of technique. Only the person who balances every technical advance with a growth in spiritual self-mastery can remain unharmed by technical progress.

In addition to the relatively indifferent techniques of the age of science, there are positively evil "techniques of degradation,"

> a whole body of methods deliberately put into operation in order to attack and destroy in human persons belonging to some definite class or other their self-respect, and in order to transform them little by little into mere human waste products, conscious of themselves as such, and in the end forced to despair of themselves, not merely at an intellectual level, but in the very depths of their souls.[29]

In general, these evil techniques operate through a person's self-image, for "man depends, to a very great degree, on the idea he has of himself, and . . . this idea cannot be degraded without at the same time degrading man."[30]

The demands for respect heard frequently today echo this thought of Marcel. The person, in contrast to the degraded *on*, is aware that she is free. And in the extreme case in which she would be in danger of being reduced by physical or psychological force to a mere automaton, her final recourse must be to the Transcendent, in an appeal

> to a level of being, an order of the spirit, which is also the level and order of grace, of mercy, of charity; and to proclaim, while there is still time, that is to say before the state's psychological manipulations have produced in us the alienation from our true selves that we fear, that we repudiate *in advance* the deeds and acts that may be obtained from us by any sort of constraint whatsoever.[31]

The ultimate guarantor of my freedom, then, can only be such a Transcendence.

The totalitarian state is antithetical to the person. It demands unquestioning obedience and swallows up every possible competitor, be it church, family, or labor union, thus making assumption of personal responsibility impossible. It is therefore up to

> each of us, within his own proper field, in his profession, to pursue an unrelaxing struggle for . . . the dignity of man. . . . It is perhaps above all in the field of law, in the field of the legal rights of the person, that this struggle ought to be carried on. . . .[32]

Against the claims of a totalitarian state such as that advocated by many marxists, Marcel holds that the notions of person and personal rights need to be maintained as our "only imaginable safeguard against a condition of technocratic barbarism which is perhaps the most hideous state of affairs we can conceive."[33]

In contrast to the human being reduced to an impersonal level by the omnicompetent state, the person is the being of honor, whose *"word is himself,"* as Marcel says, referring to Heidegger.[34] The person, in contrast to the *on*, can experience the intersubjectivity which is a basic datum of metaphysics through experiencing love (*agape*).[35] It is only the person, conscious of being in a state of captivity, who can hope and radiate hope to others.[36] It is only the person, the spiritually mature human being, who can exercise the creative fidelity which can renew "not only the person who practices it, but the recipient, however unworthy he may have been of it to start with."[37] Clearly Marcel's position on the questions of confrontation and act and the other issues discussed above grows directly out of his understanding of the meaning of person.

PROBLEM AND MYSTERY

Marcel was also deeply interested in the distinction between what he identified as problem and mystery. Here too an understanding of person is of the greatest importance.

> A problem is something which I meet, which I find complete before me, but which I can therefore lay siege to and reduce. But a mystery is something in which I myself am involved. . . .
> Just because it is the essence of mystery to be recognized or capable of recognition, it may also be ignored and actively denied.[38]

It is a property of the person, once more, as a responsible being, to recognize mystery. Marcel considers that the

> merit of existentialist philosophy, insofar as we can properly speak of such a thing at all, consists more than anything else in transcending and rejecting the mode of thought which has become incarnate in optical metaphors.[39]

Instead of finding the human being a solitary intellect facing a problematic universe, the Existentialist sees her in a situation, a world made up of the concrete circumstances of her life. It is not only the "zone of the visible," the small area in the near distance, that is given as a datum for metaphysical speculation. It is the vast area either too close to be seen or infinitely distant, the area of mystery, that we need to attend to.

From what has been said, it is evident that the person has a central position in Marcel's philosophy. Through his persistent inquiry into the human situation he is committed to helping human beings become aware of their dignity. Precisely because this notion is central, however, it is important to be quite clear about its ambiguities and difficulties.

PERSON AND PERSONALITY

Marcel notes that we may tend to confuse "person" and "personality." But for him, 'personality' refers to a "stamp, an individual imprint," an "inwardness, . . . given to us . . . through certain media which are as mysteriously transparent as the voice or the glance."[40] He considers personality thus understood to be distinct from person. The terms present "two aspects or two completely distinct levels of thought." "[I]n the act where it seemed that the person was focussed, . . . abstraction has been made of any kind of inwardness, of any rootedness."[41] Now since the person "confronts his past," should it be said that this means the "personality assuming itself"? No, since there are cases in which

> it is not altogether certain that this solution is intelligible, and in any case, . . . we know . . . that there are cases in which the person only succeeds in affirming himself by a kind of *coup d'etat* whereby he strangles whatever inwardness exists within him.[42]

Marcel is clearly reluctant to attempt to reconcile his notion of person with what he calls "personality."[43]

Marcel's insights into the notion of person could perhaps be seen as a phenomenological account of the same human being spoken of by the traditional metaphysics of the Schools. But his unwillingness to see the person as a substance makes this conclusion difficult. While it is no doubt true that to see the person as substance in the Lockean or Kantian sense of substance would probably be meaningless, it does not follow that every notion of person as substance is thereby invalidated.

CONCLUSION

There seems to be a logical circle involved in the notions of act and person as Marcel uses these notions. According to Marcel, the person is person only when he acts; and the act can be act only through a person. This raises the question: Just how does one become a person? Marcel's answer is that one becomes a person in response to the "irradiation" of another person. But this line of reasoning appears to be circular.

Finally, one wonders whether Marcel is playing on words when he speaks of the temptation to "hypostatize" the person.[44] (*Hypostasier*—the French verb— is apparently less usual than the English.) *Hypostasis*, after all (or, more exactly, the hypostasis in an intellectual nature), has classically been understood to mean the ultimate subject of (human) actions, the "doer" of intelligent works, that is, the person.[45] This paradoxical use by Marcel, who is reluctant to refer to the person as substantial, is at least surprising—like marveling that granite is hard.

Marcel wants to preserve a suppleness in his concept of person. He does not want us to be able to catch it, as it were. If we do, we lose the sense of the concept that he considers important. However, the verb he chooses to reject this procedure of false reification, i.e., "to hypostatize," is an odd term to use when talking about a *hypostasis*, a term that has been used for 1500 years to speak about the person.

Marcel, who proceeded as a phenomenologist on the problem of act and person, recognized the need for clarifying his thought even for himself, although I am not aware that he was ever able to overcome this difficulty.[46] We have no statement from Marcel about the relation of his notion of person to Aristotle's notion of substance.[47] Had Marcel turned to the ancient logic and notions of substance, some of these difficulties with his thought might not have arisen. Aristotle himself had no explicit doctrine of person, and while he does not seem to have used the term 'hypostasis' in a technical philosophical sense for 'first substance', that is, the existing individual, he did clearly distinguish the first substance or agent from his action, which is an accident.[48] John Dewey avoided this difficulty of language by steering clear entirely of the old logic with its talk of substances.

The question of *hypostasis* will be taken up in Part 2, where the sources of the word 'person' and of the various philosophical terms used to elucidate it will be considered.

NOTES

1. Paul A. Schilpp and Lewis E. Hahn, ed., *The Philosophy of Gabriel Marcel*, The Library of Living Philosophers (La Salle, IL: The Open Court Publishing Company, 1984), 436–437, 64–65, 122, 202, and 414, n. 13: "'The object is defined as being independent of the characteristics that make me be this particular person and not another person.'—*Metaphysical Journal*, p. 26."
2. Gabriel Marcel, *Homo Viator*, trans. Emma Craufurd (Chicago: Henry Regnery Company, 1951), 153.
3. Ibid., 136. The German idealist philosopher J. G. Fichte (1762–1814) claimed to deduce the Kantian categories from a consideration of such logical statements as A=A. From this he concluded to the existence of a self-positing ego (required to affirm the statement). He goes on to deduce from this premise the category of reality, and comes to the notions of opposition and limitation that introduce the categories of negation and determination. Only at the end of these deductive moves does the finite consciousness, the human ego, emerge.
4. Ibid., 137.
5. Gabriel Marcel, *Creative Fidelity*, trans. Robert Rosthal (New York: The Noonday Press, 1964), 147.
6. Ibid., 105 (my translation).
7. Ibid., 106.
8. Ibid., 107 (my translation).
9. Ibid. (my translation).
10. Ibid.
11. Ibid., 108.
12. Ibid., 109 (my translation).
13. Ibid., 110 (my translation).
14. Ibid., 111 (my translation).
15. Ibid., 112.
16. Ibid., 112. This explanation by Marcel is close to the Greek root of *prosopon*, "facing someone's eyes."
17. Ibid., 114.
18. Just what does it mean to be "in a situation"? "It is quite clear that when we say it is characteristic of man to be in a situation, we do not exclusively or even mainly envisage the fact that he occupies a position in space; however . . . certain properties which seem to be purely spatial are capable of being qualified in an increasingly inward manner."—*Creative Fidelity*, 84. A suitable location is considered of prime importance in choosing a place to live; toxic wastes have made some places uninhabitable. "Take, for example, a badly situated hotel . . . [or] a man whose situation, we say, is good. . . . In both of the foregoing examples, certain relationships which we at first tend to construe as purely external, are internalized" (86). "The moment one is involved in the order of the living being, to be situated is to be exposed to" (86–87). See the discussion in chapter 9, below, of the category "where."
19. *Creative Fidelity*, 114–15.

20. Ibid., 115 (my translation).
21. Ibid., 115–16.
22. Ibid., 116. The verb 'hypostatize' is sometimes spelled 'hypostasize' following the Greek. Used in a pejorative sense it means to make concrete what really is not (false reification).
23. Ibid., 117.
24. Ibid., 116 (my translation).
25. Ibid., 117.
26. Ibid., 117–18.
27. Schilpp and Hahn, *Philosophy of Marcel*, 581. "But my dramatic works should never be regarded as a certain kind of philosophical dialogue" (176). Earlier Marcel had declared that his plays were "essentially dramas of ideas . . . in the sphere of metaphysical thought."—*Le Seuil invisible*, 2ième édition (Paris: Bernard Grasset, Editeur, 1914), Préface, 1.
28. Gabriel Marcel, *Man Against Mass Society*, Gateway Edition, trans. G. S. Fraser (Chicago: Henry Regnery Company, 1965), 10.
29. Ibid., 42.
30. Ibid., 20.
31. Ibid., 22.
32. Ibid., 244. On the question of marxist notions of personhood, see below.
33. Marcel, *Mass Society*, 231.
34. Ibid., 252.
35. Ibid., 218.
36. Gabriel Marcel, *The Mystery of Being*, Vol. 2, trans. G. S. Fraser and René Hague (Chicago: Henry Regnery Company, 1960), 179.
37. Gabriel Marcel, *Homo Viator*, 134.
38. Marcel, *The Mystery of Being*, 1:260.
39. Marcel, *Man Against Mass Society*, 40. Marcel contrasts objects of visual perception with those, for example, of touch. To see something, I need to bring it to a focus; what is too close or too distant for proper focus can still be perceived through touch or hearing.
40. Marcel, *Creative Fidelity*, 118.
41. Ibid.
42. Ibid.
43. Thomas Aquinas uses the term 'personality' differently, to mean personhood, for example: "The form signified by this name, *person*, is not essence or nature, but personality; . . . " " . . . forma significata per hoc nomen, *persona*, non est essentia vel natura, sed personalitas; . . ." *Summa Theologiae*, 5 vols. (Ottawa: Instituti Studiorum Medievalium Ottaviensis, 1951) Part I, 39, 3, ad 4, see also Part I, Qu. 29.
44. Marcel, *Creative Fidelity*, 116.
45. *Summa Theologiae*, Part I, Qu. 29, 1 and 2. Jacques Maritain, "On the Notion of Subsistence," Appendix IV of *The Degrees of Knowledge*, trans. Gerald B. Phelan (New York: Charles Scribner's Sons, 1959), 436–7, takes up the question of what precisely constitutes the metaphysical nature of personhood.
46. Cf. A. Lalande, *Vocabulaire technique et critique de la philosophie* (Paris: Presses Universitaires de France, 1951) s.v. "Hypostasier."
    Gabriel Marcel, *Royce's Metaphysics* (trans. Virginia and Gordon Ringer; Chicago: Henry Regnery Company, 1956), 72: "Between this agent and this act there could not be, of course, the unintelligible relationship which the old metaphysical systems established between substance and its manifestations. It is in the act and

through the act that the personality, i.e., the real unity of the agent, is defined."
See also 74, 87, 93, 105, 110, 119, 135, and 169; and, in Gabriel Marcel, *Being and Having*, trans. K. Farrer, (Westminster, MD: Dacre Press, 1949), 36.

In a letter, Marcel to O'Hara, dated July 3, 1964, Marcel said, in response to an earlier version of this chapter, "I did proceed as a phenomenologist on the problem of act and person. . . . This seems to me unavoidable unless one falls back on an obsolete substantialism which has been ruled out once for all by Kant. . . . But the person is not *ephemeral*, as you seem to believe, no more than values. It does not belong to the same dimension of being as state of consciousness, as feelings which often disappear. But I feel that I shall have to take up the problem, in order to make my thought clearer, even for myself. You have indeed helped me realize the need for a further development, and I thank you for this."

47. Marcel De Corte, in his introduction to Marcel's *Position et Approches Concrètes du Mystère Ontologique* (Paris: J. Vrin, 1949), 38–9, finds that Marcel belongs to the "spiritual family" of "Christian Aristotelians."

48. Cf. A. Michel, s.v. "Hypostase," in *Dictionnaire de Théologie Catholique*, 15 vols. (Paris: Letouzey et Ane, 1903–1950) VII, l, 370: " . . . the word 'hypostasis' does not enter into the philosophical vocabulary of the Stagirite." "Nevertheless, Aristotle on many occasions studies the individual subject, seen in its ultimate completion, which is none other than the hypostasis, such as we conceive of it today." "But in the ordinary language, and Aristotle uses it in this sense, 'hypostasis' means simply what is an objective, consistent, reality, as opposed to what is is only a subjective or illusory phenomenon." " . . . le mot 'hypostasis' ne fait pas partie du langage philosophique du Stagirite." "Toutefois, Aristote étudie à plusieurs reprises le sujet individuel, envisagé dans son dernier complément, lequel n'est autre que l'hypostase, telle que nous la concevons aujourd'hui." "Mais dans le langage vulgaire, et Aristote l'emploie en ce sens, 'hypostasis' signifie simplement ce qui est réalité objective, consistante, par opposition à ce qui n'est que phénomène subjectif ou illusoire" (my translation). Is Marcel's 'act' Aristotle's '*poiein*' (*facere*)? Action is one of Aristotle's nine categories and as such would not seem capable of being reduced to substance—nor *vice versa*.

PART 2

A History of the Notion
of Person

[T]he intellectual and scientific history of western Europe is reflected in the changing fortunes of the meanings of "person" and "personality," a history which has both affected and been affected by the social struggles. . . .

—John Dewey

The following chapters offer a survey of the history of the ways 'person' has been used, from ancient times to the nineteenth century. From its Greek and Latin roots to its use in French and English today, the word has undergone changes, owing in part to the contexts in which it has been used. Since the connotations inherited from these ancient sources cling to the word even today, an understanding of these earlier roots helps make intelligible the variety of emphases the word 'person' bears.

4

Ancient Sources
of the Word 'Person'

For Greece . . . provides exact equivalents . . . *ousia* for essentia, . . . *prosopon* for persona.

—Boethius

CLASSICAL SOURCES: '*PROSOPON*' AND '*PERSONA*'

Had John Dewey consulted all the classical sources of the word 'person', he might have found that in addition to the Latin sources there was a distinct source in the Greek tradition, in which the word '*prosopon*' contributed a different set of connotations from that of the Latin '*persona*'. When the word '*prosopon*' (face) came into use in Greek (about the same time as '*persona*' in Latin), '*prosopon*' already had built into it, according to Pierre Chantraine, the notion of relationship in a physical sense: it means "facing another's eyes."[1] In contrast, the Latin, '*persona*', seems to refer to the person as agent, for example in a legal action: thus Cicero speaks of "cases" involving definite "persons, places, times, actions."[2] Along with a cluster of other meanings, e.g., mask, role, being a "personage," these meanings persist to the present day. The ancient sources of the word 'person' will now be considered in detail.

The word 'person' has been used for some 2,000 years in a variety of senses. To most speakers, 'person' probably most often implies 'body': consider "neat about one's person." The use of 'nobody' to translate the French "[*Il n'y a pas*] *personne*" testifies to the ordinary identification of 'person' with body.[3]

Over a century ago Adolf Trendelenburg, in his notes on the history of the word 'person', traced some of the classical and Old Testament roots of the word, outlined the history of its use in Roman law, noted its interest to a Church council in 362, and took up the German history of the word in, among others, Luther's Bible, Melancthon, the Augsburg Confession, and Leibniz.[4] He omitted any mention of the ancient and medieval writers who contributed

42

to the development of the notion of the person as a bodily being (e.g. Nemesius, Boethius—the latter the author of Melancthon's definition—John of Damascus or Thomas Aquinas). This omission may have occurred because Trendelenburg was primarily interested in investigating the background of Kant's principally moral usage—or because the notes, published posthumously, were simply incomplete. These notes, published in the first decade of the twentieth century with an introductory note by Rudolf Eucken, were soon translated into English and came to be recognized as a classic source for information on the history of this word.

The English word 'person', in both its Latin and Greek antecedents, has its roots in the ancient Mediterranean world about a century before the beginning of the present era.[5] Greek texts before this time might employ *anthropos, soma* (body) or *kephale* (head) in referring to the human individual. Gradually the Greek terms came to be superseded by the word *'prosopon'* (face), that is, the part of the object referred to that "faces" another, is turned "toward the eye" of another.[6] This word came to mean "mask" as well. Polybius (ca. 201–120 B.C.E.) uses 'prosopon' to mean individual or person, apparently the first such use in the extant literature.[7]

The French thinker Maurice Nédoncelle, in his study of the Greek and Latin words, says:

> The word, little by little, will become synonymous with social personality and finally with the individual or person. . . . But it will attain its last step slowly. . . . it is likely that the evolution of the Greek was influenced by the Latin.[8]

Before *persona* became current in Latin, words like *'caput'* (head), or *'homo'* (human being), served, in addition to pronouns, to designate the individual human being.

Around the time of Cicero (106–43 B.C.E.), the new Latin term, *'persona'*, came into use, with six or eight meanings, including those of the human individual and the man of special dignity, the "personage." Already at this earliest appearance two aspects of the new notion can be discerned. On one hand 'person' connotes (1) the structure of human personality, in particular the makeup of the person, and on the other, (2) the activity of the person, particularly that of self-consciousness, (at least in the sense of radical capability for this activity, for the ancients do not seem to have apprehended the abstraction "self-consciousness" in the way in which it is understood today).[9] The first of these poles may be represented by the notion of substance, the second by that of quality, relation, or action.

A series of texts from Cicero showing the multiple uses of *persona* will follow, but first, as Nédoncelle says:

> It is well to note that if most of the other technical terms of the theater are Greek words latinized, there is no instance in which one goes back to the

Greek '*prosopon*'. Mask is always '*persona.*' . . . this proves . . . that the Etruscan-Latin term, altogether independent in its origins from the Greek, had enough vigor from the start to resist the foreign influence and to impose itself. . . .[10]

A word about etymologies may be in order here. Among the various etymologies suggested for the word *persona* are to be found *per se una est* (It is one with itself), and *per se sonat* (It sounds through itself), as well as (the Greek) *peri-soma* or - *zona* (a belt around the body). All, however, are less than convincing especially because the long 'o' after the 's' is not found in any of the proposed etymologies.

An Etruscan monument dating from about 500 B.C.E. bears the inscription *Phersu* and shows a masked dancing figure. Does the inscription refer to a mask or is it a proper name? And in either case is it the ancestor of the word *persona*? Perhaps, Nédoncelle thinks, "the name of the goddess would have come to signify the mask, because in the feasts of Persepona masks would have been worn."[11]

Nédoncelle notes that the multiplication of meanings of the word *persona* happened quite rapidly:

> at the time of the Second Punic War, *persona* could signify 1. the theatrical mask; 2. an actor in a play; 3. probably a (theatrical) role; and 4. probably also already the grammatical person. . . .[12] But with Cicero, all at once, all the meanings appear. We go from the theatrical world to that of juridic and psychological social life. With him, a half-century before the Christian era, the entire gamut of later meanings can be encountered, at least in its essential outlines.[13]

Among the texts Nédoncelle cites to illustrate the meanings of *persona* in Cicero are the following:

> 1. Role in the court: . . . in my own person and with perfect impartiality I play three characters [*personas*], myself, my opponent, and the arbitrator. *De Orat.* II, xxiv, 102 [trans. E. W. Sutton, Cambridge, MA, 1959]. Can we adopt the character [*persona*] of a plaintiff and lay aside that of an accuser? *Quinct.* 45 [trans. C. D. Yonge, London, 1851].
> 2. Personage or social role: [You can] bring on stage some person [or thing and let the actor sum up the whole argument]. *De Inv.* I, 52, 99 [trans. H. M. Hubbell, 1960] . . . Exercise someone's role . . . : the person of the king.
> 3. Collective reality or dignity: It is peculiarly the property of the magistrate to bear in mind that he represents (*se gerere personam*) the state. *Off.*, 124 [trans. W. Miller].
> 4. Distinctive personality, or one of dignified status: The sentiment is in keeping with the character [*persona*]. *Off.*, I, 97 [trans. Miller]. This kind of composition, although a graceful recreation, is beneath my character [*personae*] and position. *De Fin.*, 1, 1 [trans. H. Rackham]. Medea and Atreus . . . characters [*personae*] of heroic legend [trans. H. Rackham, 1967].

5. Juridic person as opposed to things: that they bear dignities of things, of persons . . . *De Orat.*, III, 53.

6. Concrete character or personality of an individual:

a. With the genitive of the proper name: I concluded that Laelius was a fit person to whom to expound my view on friendship. *De Amic.* I, 4 [trans. W. A. Falconer]. The character [*persona*] of Staientius, now so notorious and transparent, was such as to lend itself to every suspicion of dishonour. *Cluent.* 78 [trans. H. Grose Hodge, New York, 1927].

b. With an adjective: For a personal attack on me seems always popular with the disloyal. *Ad Att.*, VIII, lld [trans. E. Winstedt, 1966]. That filthy, impure, and detested character. . . . *Qu. Rosc.*, 20 [trans. John Henry Freese, New York, 1930]. whether the part [*persona*] of a man of peace. . . . *Ad Att.* 12 [trans. E. Winstedt, New York, 1913] . . . and for that purpose I considered my own character and inclination suitable. *Ad Att.*, IX, 11 [trans. E. Winstedt]. . . .

c. Absolutely: We hold the following to be the attributes of persons: name, nature, manner of life, fortune, habit, feeling, interests, purposes, achievements, accidents, speeches made. *Inv.*, I, 34 [trans. H. M. Hubbell].

7. The philosophic notion of person, that is to say, human nature, whether insofar as it is strictly individual, or insofar as it participates in reason: We must realize also that we are invested by Nature with two characters [*personis*], as it were: one of these is universal, arising from the fact of our being all alike endowed with reason and with the superiority which lifts us above the brute. . . . The other characteristic is the one that is assigned to individuals in particular. *Off.*, I, 107 [trans. Walter Miller, 1913].[14]

Nédoncelle goes on:

Rheinfelder . . . makes the pertinent remark that the advancement of the word '*persona*' must have coincided with the unusually early disappearance of '*vir*' [male individual] in the current language, in which one already opposed '*homo*' [properly, 'mankind', or an individual human being of either gender] to '*mulier*' [woman]. *Persona* would from that time serve to replace the classic and correct sense of '*homo*.'[15]

In short, '*persona*', a young term when '*prosopon*' had been in use for some time, evolved more quickly than its Greek homologue. The former caught up with the latter, surpassed it, and probably influenced it. A little before the Christian era, it could already express the idea of human individuality more often than '*prosopon*'. But as the latter should have, it expressed this individuality in an altogether simple and empirical fashion. From the theater it went to life without going by way of the law, where the technical development of the notion is later.[16]

The Greek word '*prosopon*', with most of the same meanings as '*persona*' though apparently derived from a different root,[17] came to be applied as a technical theological term in a different way from that in which its Latin counterpart was used: Greek theologians saw [rational] '*hypostasis*' as more nearly equivalent to 'persona' than was 'prosopon'.[18] Following Schlossman, Nédoncelle summarizes:

> the Greek no doubt underwent the influence of the Latin persona and the latter must have come slightly earlier to the sense of person. . . . the Greeks invented this meaning two centuries before the Romans, but the Romans generalized its use some decades before the Greeks."[19]

From the notion of mask, the words evolved to mean personage, then role played, and, finally, the actor. From its application in the theater the notion broadened to apply more generally to life, and little by little became a synonym for social personality and finally for the individual or person in general.

The Septuagint 'prosopon' translates the Hebrew 'paneh', face, with the connotation of presence. It is likely that the idea of being face to face with someone comes into the various New Testament instances of the use of the word. "One never finds in the NT the sense of mask nor that of the moral person which one finds in Epictetus. To the sense of face, the NT adds simply that of the individual."[20]

The Second Letter to the Corinthians, 1.11, uses the expression "pollon prosopon" to mean "many persons."[21] In other places in the New Testament, the word 'prosopon' has its more usual meaning of 'face', the sense given it by the ancient physician Galen (who was well acquainted with Aristotle's physical works) a little later.

The Christian Tertullian was Galen's contemporary. Like his Stoic masters in philosophy, Tertullian groped for the notion of personality. Writing in both Greek and Latin around the year 200, he seems to have been the first of the Church Fathers to use the word 'persona'. He says:

> Now, the specific character of man is not that he is formed of clay nor is his flesh the human person as if a faculty of the soul and separate person, but it [the flesh] is a thing of altogether different substance and state, joined to the soul, however, as a possession, an instrument for the conduct of life.[22]

Before Tertullian, rhetoricians had spoken of "person, place, and time" as a means of organizing thought. Eclectic in philosophy, Tertullian witnesses to the way in which technical terms were used in his time. He seems to have given currency to the term 'substantia' in philosophy, and he exerted a powerful influence upon the development of the theological use of the term 'persona'.[23]

Some two centuries after Tertullian, the writer Nemesius, who worked in the Christian East and of whom little is known, produced a remarkable treatise On the Nature of Man.[24] The work, written in Greek, includes whole pages copied from Galen, and draws heavily upon other ancient writers, notably Aristotle and Panaetius. Nemesius combined his interest in the sense organs and mental powers of human beings with an awareness of human historicity and with an evident fascination with the distinctiveness of the human individual as this is expressed in the countenance. Nemesius's discussion of the individual human being reflected his familiarity with the Aristotelian physical treatises. This tradition was largely unknown to his contemporary Augustine and was generally unavailable in Latin before the twelfth century.

Whereas both Nemesius and Galen spoke the language of the naturalist, Augustine's preoccupation is clearly that of the rhetor, one whose profession it is to deal with words. With at best an imperfect knowledge of Aristotle's physical works, and by his own admission limited in his knowledge of Greek, Augustine sought to perfect the technical vocabulary of speculative thought.[25] He says:

> I give the name *essence* to what the Greeks call *ousia*, but which we more generally designate as *substance*.
> They indeed also call it *hypostasis*, but I do not know what different meaning they wish to give to *ousia* and *hypostasis*.[26]
> The ancients also who spoke Latin, before they had these terms which have only recently come into use, that is, essence or substance, said for them, nature.[27]
> For this is one person, this is one human being. . . .[28] . . . the souls were many—a separate soul, of course, for each person. . . .[29] And one person, that is, each individual man has these three [i.e., mind, knowledge and love] in his mind. But even if we so define man as to say: "Man is a rational substance consisting of soul and body," there is no doubt that man has a soul which is not a body, and a body which is not a soul; and, therefore, these three are not man, but belong to man or are in man.[30]

The German scholar Ludger Hölscher points out that

> there is a development in Augustine's view of the human body from his early works, written under the influence of the Platonic and Neo-Platonic conception of the body as well as of his own personal experiences, to his later more mature writings. . . .[31]

Augustine treats self-consciousness in great detail and relates it to memory in a remarkable way. Remembrance is important, in different ways, to both Plato and Aristotle. Augustine was aware of their work, though in a somewhat distant way, not having the direct access to their texts that scholars have today. Plato's "recollection" turns out to be curiously atemporal, leading the soul to a world of pure Forms. Aristotle recognizes two memories, one spiritual, the other common to human beings and to some other animals as well.[32] For Augustine, memory is a spiritual power distinct from intellect and will in human beings. It not only serves to recall the past but enables one to be aware of the present. It is the vehicle of consciousness, that by which one is able to be present to oneself.[33] Hölscher sees it in one of its forms as being a kind of "unconscious." Augustine also speaks about imagination as involving all five senses.[34]

Leontius of Byzantium, who wrote around the year 550, writes: "A hypostasis is a nature (*physis*) but a nature is not yet a hypostasis. Nature answers to the definition of being, while hypostasis implies also the idea of being *per se*; ... nature connotes the universal, while hypostasis indicates distinction from the common."[35] What is striking about the Greek writers is their awareness of strata of meanings to which the Latin language was at first unable to do justice.

BOETHIUS

Writing in Latin about the year 500, Boethius provided what was to become the classical definition of the word 'person', being commonly cited in English as late as the middle of the nineteenth century: "an individual substance of a rational nature." Like his predecessors Augustine and Tertullian, Boethius was an apologist for the Christian faith. He is said to have died a martyr for his convictions, with the result that his vast undertaking of translating Aristotle's works into Latin was not carried much beyond the logical works. Like Nemesius, Boethius was an Aristotelian who nevertheless accepted Platonic positions on many points.

In his influential treatise *Against Eutyches and Nestorius*, Boethius discusses the notions of person and substance at considerable length, showing his familiarity with Aristotelian logic and physics and explicitly dissociating himself from Cicero's first use of '*persona*' in the *De Officiis*.

> nature is a substrate of Person. . . . Person cannot be predicated apart from nature. . . . a person cannot come into being among accidents (for who can say there is any person of white or black or size?) . . .
>
> Person cannot be affirmed of bodies which have no life (for no one ever said that a stone had a person), nor yet of living things which lack sense (for neither is there any person of the tree), nor finally of that which is bereft of mind and reason (for there is no person of a horse . . .), but we say there is a person of a man. . . .
>
> there is no person of . . . man [in] . . . general; only the single persons of Cicero, Plato, or other single individuals are termed persons.
>
> Wherefore . . . we have found the definition of Person: . . . The "individual substance of a rational nature." Now by this definition we Latins have described what the Greeks call *hypostasis*. For the word person seems to be borrowed from . . . masks. . . . Greece with its richer vocabulary gives the name *hypostasis* to the individual subsistence.
>
> For a thing has subsistence when it does not require accidents in order to be, but that thing has substance which supplies to other things, accidents, . . . a substrate enabling them to be. . . .[36]

It was through these definitions of Boethius (which John Duns Scotus found too logical) that the word 'person' entered medieval and modern discussions. No doubt Boethius's "individual substance" is Aristotle's "first substance"; but Boethius himself may well have been quite Platonic in his general approach to philosophy.[37] It is to be noted that Boethius, like Tertullian and Augustine before him, was acutely conscious of the relative paucity of technical philosophical terms available to Latin speakers compared with those who spoke Greek. In the year 500 or so, the Greek words 'hypostasis' and 'subsistence' make possible a more detailed and sophisticated analysis of the meaning of 'person' than the old classical Latin would have afforded.

JOHN OF DAMASCUS

The first millenium of the history of the notion of person culminates in the work of John of Damascus, a Greek-speaking writer of the eighth century. John, son of an official of the Caliph's court, in his work *On the Orthodox Faith*, integrates the anthropology of Nemesius into a theological synthesis that anticipates the scope of the great medieval *summas*. He relies on the foundation of terms and meanings developed by earlier thinkers. Copying pages from Nemesius, he discusses the various human powers and organs; in the Philosophical Chapters, he supplies a vocabulary needed for one who would wish to discuss the Orthodox Faith. John discusses the nature of man and the universe:

> The sight organs or media of sight are the nerves leading from the brain and the eyes.[38]
> A *person* is one who by reason of his own operations and properties exhibits to us an appearance which is distinct and set off from those of the same nature as he....
> One should know that the holy Fathers used the term *hypostasis* and *person* and *individual* for the same thing, namely, that which by its own subsistence subsists of itself from substance and accidents, is numerically different, and signifies a certain one, as, for example, Peter....[39]

CONCLUSION

That there was an evolution of the notion of person from the time of Cicero to that of John of Damascus, some nine centuries later, is evident. With John there is a sustained metaphysical interest lacking in Cicero. In Boethius there is an unwillingness to see the word 'person' applied to a universal entity, as Cicero had done. The person, for Boethius, was an individual being characterized by the possession of intellectual powers of knowing. John of Damascus, in the Greek tradition, concentrates upon the physical characteristics of the human person, while carrying on a metaphysical analysis of personality that echoes that of Boethius.

The precise terminology of metaphysics is to be found again some five centuries later in the great medieval thinkers, especially Thomas Aquinas, who inherited John's interest in systematic thought as well as his appreciation of Aristotelian philosophy.

NOTES

1. Pierre Chantraine, *Dictionnaire Étymologique de la Langue Grecque*, T. III (Paris: C. Klincksieck, 1974). He finds a relation between '*prosopon*' and the Sanskrit '*pratika*' with the meaning of visage or appearance.
2. Cicero *Topics* XXI, 80.
3. Jacques Barzun, *On Writing, Editing, and Publishing* (Chicago: University of Chicago Press, 1986) discusses 'personne' and its English counterpart.
4. "A Contribution to the History of the Word Person: A Posthumous Treatise by Adolf Trendelenburg," trans. Carl H. Haessler, *The Monist*, 20 (1910): 336–63. The German original was published in *Kant-Studien* in 1908 from notes dated January 20, 1870. Dewey's Hegelian mentor, George Morris, had studied with Trendelenburg.
5. See Maurice Nédoncelle, "Prosopon et Persona dans l'Antiquité Classique: Essai de Bilan Linguistique," *Revue des Sciences Religieuses*, 22 (1948): 277–99. See also his *The Personalist Challenge: Intersubjectivity and Ontology*, trans. François C. Gérard and Francis F. Burch in *The Pittsburgh Theological Monograph Series*, Vol. 27 (Allison Park, PA: Pickwick Publications, 1984). Further reflections on the history of the word 'person' are found in M. Nédoncelle, *Explorations Personnalistes* (Paris: Aubier, 1957), the first three parts of which consider Semitic and other language groups in relation to Greek and Latin. It has been claimed that the Sanskrit '*purusa*' is equivalent to the European 'person', but this seems unlikely, in that '*purusa*' answers rather to '*vir*' (male): the bridegroom is called the '*purusa*', for example. See Richard De Smet, S. J., "Towards an Indian View of the Person," *Contemporary Indian Philosophy*, Series 2, 52, and also "The Rediscovery of the Person," *Indian Philosophical Quarterly*, 4 (April 1977): 413–26. No attempt is made here to be complete in the survey of ancient and Patristic writers who used the word 'person' in a philosophical sense.
6. G. L. Prestige, *God in Patristic Thought* (London: S.P.C.K., 1959) points out that "prosopon was a non-metaphysical term for 'individual', while hypostasis was a more or less metaphysical term for 'independent object'" (179). "The ground idea of hypostasis . . . is the active sense of support or resistance." "hypostasis has come to signify endurance and stiffening, or brass-fronted impudence" (170). René Braun, *"Deus Christianorum": Recherches sur le vocabulaire doctrinale de Tertullien* (Paris: Presses Universitaires de France, 1962), 171, says that Seneca used *hypostasis* in the sense of Stoic physics, for something real, material; "It was only with Quintillian that a new, entirely different, sense appeared, that of 'essence', or of 'nature.'" The original sense of the word, as used by Aristotle, seems to have been simply "sediment."
7. Polybius *The Histories* 6 vols., trans. W. R. Paton, The Loeb Classical Library (Cambridge: Harvard University Press, 1974), Vol. 4, XV, 25.26: "They had no leader [*prosopon*]." "Face," "mask," and "front" are among other meanings of the term in the numerous instances of Polybius's use of it.
8. Maurice Nédoncelle, "Prosopon et Persona . . .", 281–282.
9. See William Telfer, ed., *Cyril of Jerusalem and Nemesius of Emesa* (London: S.C.M. Press, 1955), 297, n. 2, and 322, n. 14.
10. Nédoncelle, "Prosopon et Persona . . .", 295–96.
11. Nédoncelle, Ibid., 175.
12. '*Purusa*' appeared in Sanskrit grammar around this time, with the sense of the three grammatical persons of the verb inflection. See also Ludolf Malten, *Die Sprache des Menschlichen Antlitzes im Frühen Griechentum* (Berlin: Walter de Gruyter, 1961), 2.
13. Nédoncelle, "Prosopon et Persona," 296–97.

14. See Christopher Gill, "Personhood and Personality: the Four-*personae* theory in Cicero, *De Officiis*, I," in Julia Annas, ed., *Oxford Studies in Ancient Philosophy*, Vol. 6, (Oxford: Clarendon Press, 1988), 169–99, for a study of Cicero's theory (and its dependence upon Panaetius) of the *persona* common to all human beings—involving rationality—that peculiar to one individual, that of one's social position, and that resulting from the choice of a life work (174). Seneca, *Epistle XVIII*, 15 and *XXIV*, 13, uses *persona* to mean "mask" and also "human being."

15. Nédoncelle, "Prosopon et Persona. . . .", 298.

16. Nédoncelle, "Prosopon et Persona. . . .", 299. See also René Braun, *"Deus Christianorum:"*, 228–36 and 553 on Tertullian's use of '*persona*' as independent of the later legal use (contrary to Rheinfelder). Tertullian's usage adopted the "everyday language associated with the word *persona*—which designated the individual human being (especially by name) and was manifested in action and word" (my translation).

17. '*Pros*' and '*ops*' 'toward the eye': the face is what is turned toward the eye of another. See also Chantraine, and, on the Latin word, F. P. Leverett, *A New and Copious Lexicon of the Latin Language* (Philadelphia: J. B. Lippincott Company, 1893); P. G. W. Glare, *Oxford Latin Dictionary* (Oxford: Clarendon Press, 1976); and Ludolf Malten, *Die Sprach des Menschlichen Antlitzes im Fruehen Griechtum* (Berlin: Walter de Gruyter & Co., 1961).

18. See René Braun, *"Deus Christianorum:"* "In his definitive vocabulary of the doctrine of the Trinity, Tertullian uses *persona* to indicate what, in the intimate life of God, characterizes and distinguishes; he expresses by *substantia* that which brings together and unites" (238; my translation). See also 239–42, and Prestige, 188: " . . . hypostasis regularly emphasizes the externally concrete character of the substance, or empirical objectivity."

19. Nédoncelle, "Prosopon et Persona. . . .", 168.

20. Nédoncelle, Ibid., 167.

21. Vulgate: "*ex multorum personis.*" See also Braun, *Deus Christianorum*, 559, for the Hebrew influence upon New Testament Greek.

22. Tertullian, *On the Soul*, trans. Edwin A. Quain, in *Tertullian, Apologetical Works and Minucius Felix, Octavius*, trans. R. Arbesmann, S. E. J. Daly, and E. A. Quain, *The Fathers of the Church*, Vol. 10 (New York: The Fathers of the Church, 1950), 40, 272.

23. See Braun, *"Deus Christianorum."*

24. See William Telfer, ed., Nemesius, *On the Nature of Man*, 44, in *Cyril of Jerusalem and Nemesius of Emesa*, Vol. 4, The Library of Christian Classics (Philadelphia: The Westminster Press, 1955), 429–30.

25. See St. Augustine, *The Trinity*, trans. Stephen McKenna (Washington, DC: The Catholic University of America Press, 1963), III, Preface. Augustine's thought evolved during the course of his life, as attested by his book of *Retractations*, in which he corrects some of his earlier formulations. On Augustine's early view of man, see Robert J. O'Connell, *St. Augustine's Early Theory of Man, A.D. 386–391* (Cambridge, MA: The Belknap Press, 1968), 262: "The original sense of *persona* as referring to an analogue of the theatrical face-mask is very much to the fore in Augustine's thought in this period."

26. Augustine *On the Trinity* V, 8, (9–10), 187. See also VII, 6, (11), 235: "Although they [the Greeks] could also call the three persons three *prósopa* if they wished, just as they call the three substances three *hypostases*, yet they preferred that term [hypostases], perhaps because it was more in accordance with the usage of their language."

27. Ibid., VII, 6, (11), 238. See also V, 8, for his discussion of the word 'person'.

28. Ibid., XII, 12, (18), 361.
29. Ibid., XIII, 2, (5), 375.
30. Ibid., XV, 7, (11), 464–5. Augustine makes the important observation that in God " . . . nothing is said according to accident, because there is nothing changeable in Him, nor does everything that is said of Him refer to His substance. For something can be said of Him in regard to relation."—*On the Trinity* V, 5, (6), 179–80. See also ibid., VII, 4, (8), 232: "For person is a generic name, so much so, in fact, that even man can be so called in spite of the great distance between man and God." Hubertus R. Drobner, *Person-Exegese und Christologie bei Augustinus* (Leiden: E. J. Brill, 1986), 117, sees the year 411 as marking Augustine's first use of 'person' to refer to the human composite of soul and body, an evolution of his doctrine of the unity of the human being from an earlier position, influenced by Neoplatonism, that the union of soul with body was accidental.
31. Ludger Hölscher, *The Reality of the Mind: Augustine's Philosophical Arguments for the Human Soul as a Spiritual Substance* (New York: Routledge & Kegan Paul, 1986), 29.
32. See Aristotle's *On Memory and Recollection* and *Metaphysics* 1, 1.
33. Augustine *On the Trinity* XIV, 11, (14), 432: "But whoever says that memory is not concerned with present things, let him take note how this is expressed in secular literature . . . : ' . . . nor did the Ithacan forget himself in so great a danger.' Now when Vergil says that Ulysses did not forget himself, what else did he mean except that he remembered himself? Since, then, he was present to himself, he would not have remembered himself at all, unless memory pertained to present things. Wherefore, as in past things, that is called memory which makes it possible for them to be recalled and remembered, so in a present thing, which the mind is to itself, that is not unreasonably to be called memory, by which the mind is present to itself, so that it can understand its own thought, and both can be joined together by the love of itself." And XV, 21, (40), 507: "for the understanding which appears in thought comes from the understanding which already existed in the memory but was latent there, although even thought itself, unless it had some memory of its own, would not return to those things which it had left in the memory when it thought of other things." Cf. Charles E. Scott, "Consciousness and the Conditions of *Consciousness*," *The Review of Metaphysics*, 25, 4 (June 1972): 164: "as one intends, he has a sense for the past, an immediate consciousness of pastness, . . . which is part of every intention's fabric." In the mid-nineteeth century, Alphonse Gratry, in his philosophy of the person, emphasized the notion of the "root of the soul," a third intellectual power in addition to intellect and will.
34. Hölscher, *Mind*, 48; Augustine, *On the Trinity*, XV, 11, (20).
35. Leontius Byzantinus, *Contra Nestorianos et Eutychianos, Patrologia Graeca*, ed. J.-P. Migne, Vol. 86–1 (Paris: J.-P. Migne, 1860), 1 (1279–80A).
36. Boethius, *A Treatise Against Eutyches and Nestorius*, Part II, 83–III, 89, in *The Theological Tractates*, trans. H. F. Stewart and E. K. Rand (New York: G. P. Putnam's Sons, 1926).
37. See M.-D. Chenu, *Nature, Man, and Society in the Twelfth Century: Essays on New Theological Perspectives in the Latin West*, trans. Jerome Taylor and Lester K. Little (Chicago: The University of Chicago Press, 1963), 74.
38. Saint John of Damascus, *Writings*, trans. Frederic H. Chase Jr., *The Fathers of the Church*, Vol. 37 (New York: The Fathers of the Church, 1958), *The Orthodox Faith*, Book II, Chapter 18, 242–3.
39. Ibid., *The Fount of Knowledge*, Chap. 43, 67–8.

5

Medieval and Early Modern
Views of Person

... [M]y purpose ... is to make precise the meaning of the word
'person'. . . .

—Richard of Saint Victor

A CONVERSATION ABOUT PERSONS

Richard of Saint Victor was, like other medieval writers on personhood, interested in the theological aspects of the question.[1] But because theologians more or less consciously use philosophical reasoning in their speculations, his doctrine of personality is important for the history of the philosophical use of this term. Thomas Aquinas, fortunate in his fresh access to most of Aristotle's works, clearly differentiated philosophy from theology, while putting the former at the service of the latter.

By the time of John Duns Scotus, working around the beginning of the fourteenth century, the great battle over the acceptance of Aristotle's philosophical ideas had in large part been won. A voluntarist and a dedicated follower of Augustine, Scotus deprecated Plato's and Aristotle's concern with universals, and he carried on a dialogue with earlier thinkers like John of Damascus and other thinkers of the East—Christian, Jewish, Muslim, and pagan alike—a world of thinkers largely unknown a century earlier.

Scotus adopted a univocal theory of being, unlike Aquinas who put forth an analogical theory of how one should speak of God and creatures. Scotus therefore needed a theory of divine Persons that would apply, as regards its fundamental metaphysics, to human persons as well. Thomas taught that there is only an analogous likeness between God and creatures: there is, in his opinion, more difference than likeness, even in qualities like goodness that might be said to be common to God and the creature.

In the seventeenth century, the early English philosopher Thomas Hobbes drew upon the Latin sources for 'person', finding it congenial for his political theory. He was in touch with the traditional understanding of the word 'person' in its Greek as well as its Latin root and with something of its history.

These thinkers, (and those already considered in Chapter 4), carried on a kind of dialogue with one another over the centuries, a dialogue to which thinkers today contribute. Each will be considered in what follows.

A NEW TECHNICAL VOCABULARY

According to the historian Chenu,

> several definitions of the masters . . . gained currency toward the end of the twelfth century and afterwards, and they became part of the standard curriculum even though they sometimes stirred up controversy. . . . Such was the case with their definition of person: "A hypostasis distinguished by its property. . . ."[2]

The renewal of learning that took place in Europe in the twelfth century called into question the meaning of ancient texts that had, in some cases, lain unopened for half a millenium in places like monastic libraries where they had escaped pillage by successive waves of marauders during the centuries following the fall of the Roman Empire.

Universities arose at Paris, Oxford, and throughout Europe, to provide clerics with theological learning adequate to the new development of culture. A feature of this new learning was its emphasis upon human beings not as souls, angels, or purely intellectual beings of some sort, but as part of nature.

To be able to discuss the new questions, however, a new vocabulary had to be developed. Chenu says:

> The most questionable terms lost their ambiguity precisely because of the hard work of theologians and thus became useful instruments for the solution of new problems. The term *persona* is the leading instance of this, for it became universally understood and settled, not only that the term was legitimate, but that it had a definition, even though it was variously elaborated. Instead of *subsistentia*, which was henceforth currently used, Richard of St. Victor preferred less learned terms; yet he did not object to its use by specialists. "The word 'person' is on the lips of everyone, even rustics," he said.[3]

RICHARD OF SAINT VICTOR

The great problem for all medieval writers was to become clear about the sources of their pronouncements: was it a theological, Scripture-based opinion, or one derived from the secular learning (and from what Richard of Saint Victor calls "experience") amassed over the ages?[4] Richard, writing in the late twelfth century, was mostly interested in the theology of the divine Trinity, and in how the doctrines of Trinity and Incarnation were expressed in different ways in East and West.[5] He was interested in the person as a being related to God. But speaking of the mysteries required the use of human referents that he proceeded to develop.

> The word 'person' is used by everyone, even people without learning; the word 'subsistence', on the contrary, is not even known to all the educated. . . . It is then the simple and common idea that the word 'person' arouses in every mind that will be my point of departure.[6]
>
> As regards individual substantiality, that is what is found in one sole individual exclusively and can absolutely not be common to many substances. We do not have a word in use to designate an individual substantiality; but for clarity's sake we can create a term derived from a proper name. Let us say then the 'danielity' from the name 'Daniel'. . . . Thus danielity must be understood as that substantiality itself, or if you prefer that subsistence, which makes Daniel that substance which he is and in which no one else can participate. Hence, while humanity, like bodiliness, is common to a great number of beings, danielity is absolutely incommunicable, in this sense that it belongs to him in such a way as to be incapable of belonging to another.[7]
>
> For a human being is composed of a body and of a soul and the two together are but one person. . . . here there is plurality of persons in the unity of substance. . . .[8]

Richard here makes clear, in trying to establish a vocabulary suited to theological use, that one common humanity ('substance') is found distributed among many individual human beings. But their individuality is such that while the substance or human nature common to all is "communicated" to each individual, the personhood or "danielity" of Daniel—*his* individual substance or subsistence—is not able to be shared with another human being.

'Communication' here does not refer primarily to speech; it is a technical term (like 'subsistence', which in the technical medieval theological vocabulary refers to metaphysical issues, and in modern usage refers to economic issues in phrases like "a subsistence wage"). Incommunicability in this setting refers to the inalienability of personhood: my being myself cannot be given to or taken from me, any more than my finger prints can become those of another.[9]

Subsistence and incommunicability do not for Richard imply fixity, however, nor perfectly unitary existence:

> the same person . . . can grow or diminish or become unequal to itself. . . . in the person, power, wisdom, and justice are not identical. . . . Consider power, for example: you know that this is easy, that difficult, that impossible. . . .[10]
>
> Let us begin by saying again, following others, that the term 'person' is in the line of substance, makes one think of substance. There is nonetheless a great difference between the two terms.[11]

Animals are substances, and to be human involves being a substance. But more is involved in the use of 'person'.

But one never says 'person' except of a rational substance. Furthermore, when we use the word 'person', we always mean but one sole substance, one and singular. . . . And so, in certain cases a generic property is understood; in others, a specific property; and with the word 'person', an individual, singular, incommunicable property is understood.[12]

Note well that the word 'substance' signifies not so much someone as something; on the contrary, the word 'person' designates rather someone than something. . . . When one says: "What is it?" one asks about a common property; when one says: "Who is it?" one asks about a singular property.[13] In a human being, the body is one substance, the soul is another substance, and yet there is but one person. In human nature one sole and same person is, under different headings, bodily and incorporeal, visible and invisible, mortal and immortal; nevertheless the unity of the person is maintained despite such a diversity of substances.[14]

Certainly, each human person possesses a singular nature proper to him and that distinguishes him from every other. . . . And when several have the same father, they do not come from the same element of the paternal substance.[15]

What is proper to humankind is to possess substantial being at once by propagation and by creation, since the flesh is transmitted and the soul is created.

As for incommunicable existence, it is that which can belong to but one sole person.[16]

Richard criticizes the definition of Boethius ("an individual substance of a rational nature") principally on theological grounds: while it might hold of human persons, it seems ill-suited to the divine. There is a difference between the East and the West in the way 'substance' and 'subsistence' are used. Richard claims that "it is more precise to call persons 'existences' rather than substances or subsistences."[17] Accepting the etymology of 'existence' to mean a "standing out from" something else, he thinks he has found a better definition of person: "every created person is . . . an individual existence of a rational nature."[18]

Richard here intends to emphasize that existence implies a relationship between the person's substantial being or subsistence and the person's source or origin. A person not only exists, but exists in virtue of a relationship of origin. For Richard, this definition brings out an essential property of persons that Boethius' definition did not express.

Ewert Cousins explains the importance of this idea of relation for the essence of Richard's teaching:

Richard's treatment of charity involves three propositions: (1) charity is a perfection, and, in fact, the greatest perfection; (2) it must be shared in also by God; (3) charity, which involves love for another person, is superior to self-love.

This principle . . . contains also one of his most penetrating insights into the nature of the human person. Self-transcendence, not self-love is the highest perfection and as such reveals the nature of the person.[19]

love for another person produces happiness and presupposes generosity. . . . happiness connotes, and presupposes . . . the individuality or incommunicability of the person.[20]

Although Richard's thought is essentially dynamic, Cousins believes he "uses the static structures of Aristotelian dialectic," and does not explore to the extent one might have hoped the relatedness of human persons to one another. Quite different from Richard is the scholastic theologian and philosopher Thomas Aquinas.

THOMAS AQUINAS

The great intellectual divide between Richard of Saint Victor and Thomas Aquinas was created by the rediscovery in the thirteenth century of the bulk of the works of Aristotle by philosophers in the West. Thomas and his contemporaries turned eagerly to the study of Aristotle's writings, finding there a plan of scientific work unknown to Europeans since the end of the Roman Empire.[22]

Having a grasp of Aristotle's physical and metaphysical doctrines enabled Thomas to distinguish clearly the realms of thought in which he himself operated. For him, as for Aristotle, the knowledge of the natural world, or "physics" (including a number of subsidiary disciplines such as studies of the anatomy and the movement of animals), was naturally presupposed to the study of all being—called "metaphysics" from the time of the first editing of Aristotle's works.

The domain of philosophy itself includes all being, looked at from the particular point of view of natural human powers of knowing. The discipline of theology relies on sources of knowledge distinct from those of the philosophical sciences. Thomas was able to work with both Greek and Roman theological traditions as well as the rediscovered Aristotelian philosophy, without confusing these distinct fields.

In treating of the notion of person in a formal way, therefore (in contrast to the myriad instances of his less formal use of the term), Thomas had to deal with the theology of the Trinity and the Incarnation and at the same time to set forth a definition of the term useful for the human sciences.

Thomas in his epistemology distinguishes between "intellect" and "reason": "intellect" emphasizes such effortless uses of the mind as insight; "reason" applies to the laborious use of the mind for problem solving in disciplines like mathematics. He had no problem, however, with accepting Boethius's definition of 'person', despite the possibility of its being misinterpreted as attributing an unbecoming laboriousness to the working of the divine mind.[23]

Thomas could accommodate that definition, perhaps, because of another feature of his philosophy: analogical predication. Aristotle had already noted that a term could be equivocal or univocal.[24] Thomas taught that many terms, such as 'goodness', could be applied to various things in such a way that although the term was correctly applied to two different things, like a cat and a dog, it was in virtue of different qualities that it was applied to each: the term 'good' could be applied to both a dog and a cat; but the qualities that make a dog good are not those that make a cat such. The dog and cat are more different than alike, and yet, 'goodness' is properly applied to both. Each does really "partake" of goodness.

Analogy applies most of all to predications about God and creatures: whatever is said of God must be understood as applying to God in a way infinitely different from the way in which it applies to any creature. God's goodness is infinitely beyond any goodness of a human being. Through this analogical means of knowing, God is known imperfectly; but even a little knowledge of God is better than precise knowledge of creatures. Thus, the word 'rational' in the definition of 'person' could be understood in a generous spirit as applying to God as well as human persons.[25]

Augustine had seen that in God " . . . nothing is said according to accident, because there is nothing changeable in Him, nor does everything that is said of Him refer to His substance. For something can be said of Him in regard to relation."[26] For Thomas, the divine Persons are subsistent relations: he combines the notion of substance and that of relation into one notion appropriate to God.[27]

When he speaks of human persons, Thomas makes it clear that it is the substantial composite of body and soul, never the soul alone, that is the person. Unlike Richard who says, "the body is one substance, the soul is another substance," Thomas is careful to point out that these two are, as it were, ingredient in the composite human being who is a person, even though it is possible for the soul to exist, at death, apart from the body, as a spiritual being, but not the complete person; and personality bespeaks completeness. Personality is in fact the ultimate completion of the composite human person.

In his early *Commentary on the Sentences*, Thomas considers the characteristics of personality in a number of places. He makes it clear that the person is the complete being, a whole in relation to that person's individual nature, composite of matter and form:

> person is that reality [*hoc aliquid*] which subsists in that nature. . . . humanity [*homo*] does not subsist, but this man, to whom belongs the notion of the person. It belongs to the notion of person therefore that it be a distinct subsistent thing, . . . including everything in the thing; but nature includes only the essentials.
> . . . not only from the soul does the human being [*homo*] have the quality

of personhood [*quod sit persona*], but from it and also from the body; for one subsists from both.[28]

. . . the individual of a rational nature is said to be a person;[29]

person . . . signifies a substance that is a hypostasis.[30]

. . . person . . . signifies the reality itself. . . .[31]

More than a refinement of expression separates Thomas from Richard and from the other great medieval thinkers. Thomas alone among them adopted the principle that there is a real distinction between essence (what something is) and its actualizing existence (the fact that it is) as the fundamental principle of his metaphysics.[32]

In doing so, he made clear the contingency of every creature and its radical dependence upon the source of its being.

For the division of nature into many persons among human beings occurs partly because of the imperfection of human nature, which is not its own existence, and also partly from the mode of distinctness, because human persons are distinguished by matter, which is part of the essence.[33]

According to some philosophers, Thomas places the essence of personhood precisely in the act of existence. For others, it is to be found rather in a unique receptivity for this existence.[34] In any case, personhood is at its deepest level a positive entity.

To speak of the person in this way is to imply that the highly unitary person is nonetheless a highly composite being, both physically and metaphysically. For reasons that need not be gone into here, Thomas endorses Aristotle's theory of matter-form (that is, in this case, body-soul) composition of every material thing. This implies that the form (or, in living things, the soul) gives existence to the potentially existing matter, making what is the matter of the soil, for example, into the matter of a plant, as the requisite physical changes take place.

Beneath all physical changes, however, Thomas finds, as Aristotle had not, a metaphysical distinction between *what* something is and *that* it is: between essence and existence in every created thing.[35] He sees, using Aristotelian terms, the essence as potential to existence, in a way analogous to the relation of matter to form. And he sees personhood as involving, for example, my individual essence and the individual existence I am given by God.

Thomas tersely expresses his understanding of what it means to be a human person.

'Person' means that which is most perfect in the whole of nature, namely, what subsists in rational nature. . . . Since in comedies and tragedies famous men were represented, this name 'person' came to be used in reference to men of high rank. . . . To subsist in rational nature is a characteristic implying dignity, and hence . . . every individual with rational nature is called 'person'.[36]

... person in any kind of nature, signifies what is distinct in that nature. For instance, used of human nature, it refers to *this* flesh, *these* bones and *this* soul, which are the sources of man's individuality; these are indeed part of what is meant by 'a human person'. . . .[37]

This name 'person' is used to signify the subsisting thing in a certain nature.[38]

The form signified by the name 'person' is not essence or nature, but personality.[39]

Thomas refers to Richard of Saint Victor's definition of 'person' in the course of developing his own ideas in his *Summa*. He notes, but without extended comment, that Richard's formulation involves regarding a negation as the ultimate expression of personality.[40] As a member of the newly founded Dominican order, Thomas left behind him a school of thinkers who appreciated and developed his thought. Several decades later, John Duns Scotus, also a member of a religious order, the Franciscans, stood at the head of a long line of Scotist thinkers who at one time were said to outnumber all other groups put together. Like Richard, but unlike Thomas, Scotus saw personality as involving fundamentally negative principles.

JOHN DUNS SCOTUS

John Duns Scotus, though he died a young man and was unable to complete his monumental work, nevertheless expounded a remarkable theological and metaphysical system that in many respects challenged Thomistic views. He calls what is only possible, "being," and in this way he emphasizes the thrust of being, thus understood, toward its completion. He prefers Richard's definition, that "a person is the 'incommunicable existence of an intellectual nature'" to that of Thomas and Boethius. He says that it is to be preferred to the Boethian definition because, he thinks, the latter could be applied to the soul, "which is unbecoming."[41]

The reason for the unfittingness is that the "soul is that by which something is, but is not itself that thing."[42] And so, after death, the soul apart from the body is not, strictly speaking, a person until such time as it is reunited with its body. There is a "twofold incommunicability" in reference to the person: it cannot be another, and it has no aptitude (or thrust) to be communicated or joined to another in the way, for example, that the soul is to the body.

In taking over Richard's definition, however, Scotus gave it his own characteristic emphasis. More than a century stood between Richard and Scotus; from the era of Thomas, Scotus inherited a philosophical library in which Aristotle was no longer a novelty; and over the years there had been a change in the nature of the philosophical and theological questions being considered.

Thomas had carefully studied the Aristotelian logic; Scotus shows himself a master of intricate logical distinctions, and differs from Thomas on numerous physical and metaphysical points. Underlying Scotus's doctrine of the person is the principle that theology is practical, aiming at the happiness of the individual. Doctrine that gives prominence to theory, science, logic, that is, to the general, is, Scotus thinks, unsatisfactory as an ultimate ground for knowledge about an individual's search for happiness.

For Scotus, being is univocally predicated of both finite being and infinite being.[43] In including the possible as part of his notion of "being," Scotus postulates a "being" that is as it were "thin," barely existent. Like Richard's (and Thomas's), Scotus's human person is both subsistent and related to the originating Creator. Like Thomas, whose *Summa of Theology* is organized on a circular (Neoplatonic) basis of procession from and return to God, Scotus emphasizes the human person as embarked upon a career in time and space that will lead to the fruition of human life in the attainment of a divine goal. But Scotus's voluntarism contrasts with Thomas's intellectualism. Scotus emphasizes a finite being with a thrust toward self-realization, self-possession, that calls for ever greater self-determination. It is a history, for human persons, of growth toward the greatest possible freedom.

The Christian doctrine of the Incarnation specifies that a divine Person took on a complete human nature but no human person. Human personality, according to Scotus, must therefore be something that is not a positive, integral part of the individual human nature.

For Scotus, therefore, personhood in a human being is constituted by a double negation: denial of being taken up by another person and denial even of the habitual tendency or inclination (aptitude, disposition) to be so taken up or assumed. While being nothing positive, this twofold negation of actual and aptitudinal "communication" to another person suffices to constitute the "ultimate solitude" that is the human person. The person thus constituted is made a "this" (*haec*), not, as Thomas might say, thanks to the designated matter of which it is made (a bodily occasion for individuation), but by an additional form, called by Scotus "thisness" (*haecceitas*).[44] The ultimate "thisness" of the existing thing can, finally, be grasped in a direct (but vague) act of intellectual intuition, at the same time as the intellect acquires, thanks to abstraction, a generalized knowledge of the nature of the thing known. Scotus's direct intellectual intuition of the individual is unknown to the epistemology of Thomas or Aristotle.[45]

The poet Gerard Manley Hopkins greatly appreciated Scotus's emphasis upon the uniqueness of the individual. Scotus's marking *haecceitas* as a final note of individuality foreshadows, in some ways, Locke's emphasis upon personal identity. Scotus says:

> as created nature is to singularity, so must intellectual nature at least be to personality. But created nature is singular in such a way that it cannot remain the same without its singularity; therefore neither can the singular

intellectual nature remain the same without its personality.[46]
... magnitude pertains more to essence as it is understood apart from person, than action or passion, which cannot be without the supposit; ...[47]

For Scotus, the personhood of a human being results from the fact that this individual human nature, like every nature in Aristotle's system (although Aristotle never descended to the detailed discussion on this point that interested Scotus), has a thrust toward its completion and perfection in actuality. The individual nature has, therefore, an "aptitude or disposition" for its own completion. In the absence of anything that would impede its completion, the singular individual intelligent nature is completed actually and thus is a person. Personality, for Scotus, consists ultimately in two negations: that of actual and of aptitudinal "communication" of an individual human nature to another for its personal being.

> Therefore, we can say that the formal reason our nature is invested with a created personality is not something positive; for in addition to singularity we find no positive entity that renders the singular nature incommunicable. All that is added to singularity is the negation of dependence or incommunicability, the denial that it is given over to someone.[48]

The human person, nevertheless, is always a related being, not some impossibly isolated substance.

In his subtle penetration into the metaphysical structure of the person, Scotus took the analysis of personality in a different direction from that of Thomas; he also consciously repudiated the Boethian definition, which to Scotus was not sufficiently explicit to apply to persons in an unambiguous way. Lacking Thomas's real distinction between essence and existence, he saw personality as consisting ultimately in a twofold negation: of actual and aptitudinal assumption by another person. And so Scotus, writing in the fourteenth century, reached back beyond the thirteenth-century doctors to Richard of Saint Victor, whose definition of person he sees as completing and correcting that of Boethius.

Quite different from these medieval thinkers was the early modern philosopher Thomas Hobbes. Yet he was able to see the question of the person in the ancient and medieval contexts in a way that became increasingly difficult for later thinkers.

THOMAS HOBBES

The Scotist school enjoyed its greatest influence in the seventeenth century at the very time that Thomas Hobbes was writing his treatise on the origin of the state, *Leviathan*.[49] In it he discusses the person as a legal agent, referring to the one responsible for his action, its author. The notion of the person as agent is essential to his argument for the existence of the state as the effect of human agency. He also briefly mentions the Greek word *prosopon*, 'face'.

Hobbes distinguished a "natural" from a "feigned" person. The "natural person" is one whose words or acts are considered his own; the "feigned or artificial person" is one whose words or acts are owned by another. He says:

A PERSON is he whose words or actions are considered, either as his own, or as representing the words or actions of another man, or of any other thing to whom they are attributed, whether truly or by fiction. . . .

The word *person* is Latin, instead whereof the Greeks have *prosopon*, which signifies the face, as *persona* in Latin signifies the *disguise* or *outward appearance* of a man, counterfeited on the stage; and sometimes more particularly that part of it which disguiseth the face, as a mask or vizard: and from the stage hath been translated to any representer of speech and action, as well in tribunals as theatres. So that a person is the same that an actor is, both on the stage and in common conversation; and to personate is to act or represent himself or another; and he that acteth another is said to bear his person, or act in his name (in which sense Cicero useth it where he says . . . I bear three persons; my own, my adversary's, and the judge's), and is called . . . a representer or representative. . . .

Of persons artificial, some have their words and actions owned by those whom they represent. And then the person is the *actor*, and he that owneth his words and actions is the *author*, in which case the actor acteth by authority. . . .[50]

A multitude of men are made *one* person when they are by one man, or one person, represented. . . .

Dugald Stewart describes the situation in this way: "In consequence of this transference of natural rights to an individual, or to a body of individuals, the multitude becomes *one* person. . . ."[51] It was upon this notion of an "artificial person," the result of the "transference of natural rights to an individual or . . . a body of individuals" that Hobbes constructed his theory of the state. Hobbes's purpose was different from that of his theological predecessors, despite his own interest in integrating theological as well as other data into his political philosophy. John Dewey's doctrine of person echoes that of Hobbes in its emphasis upon human agency and representation.

CONCLUSION

Each of the thinkers discussed in this chapter tried to clarify the notion of human personhood through a discussion of the term 'person' that took account of its roots in the usage of earlier thinkers. With the coming of the modern period, a revulsion against earlier thought, particularly that of the medieval period immediately preceding it, led to a gradual loss of the traditional ideas about the nature of human personality. By the late eighteenth century, a curious confusion about the use of the word 'person', as Boethius had defined it, becomes evident.

NOTES

1. No attempt is made here at a complete survey of all medieval writers who spoke of the person. Rather, the purpose of this chapter is to give an idea of the sorts of things that interested a few of the thinkers whose thought still resonates with people today. For a careful study of theologians whose thought includes philosophical arguments and who provide the milieu for thinkers like Thomas Aquinas and John Duns Scotus, see Walter H. Principe's four volumes on "The Theology of the Hypostatic Union in the Early Thirteenth Century," for example, Vol. I, *William of Auxerre's Theology of the Hypostatic Union* (Toronto: Pontifical Institute of Mediaeval Studies, 1963).

2. M.-D. Chenu, *Nature, Man, and Society in the Twelfth Century: Essays on New Theological Perspectives in the Latin West*, trans. Jerome Taylor and Lester K. Little (Chicago: The University of Chicago Press, 1963), 285–6.

3. Richardi a Sancto Victore, *De Trinitate* (*Opera Omnia*, Paris: J.-P. Migne, *Patrologiae Cursus Completus, Patrologia Latina*, Series Secundus, 1855), 196, 933. "Nomen personae in ore omnium, etiam rusticorum, versatur...." IV, 4. Chenu, *Nature, Man, and Society*, 34. Richard (died 1173) belonged to the Canons Regular, a new group at that time, in Paris.

4. Richard de Saint-Victor, *La Trinité*, trans. Gaston Salet (Paris: Les Editions du Cerf, 1959) 3, 9, 187; 4, 3, 233; 2, 12, 131.

5. On the complicated question of the meaning of "East," some helpful remarks are to be found in David B. Burrell, "Aquinas and Islamic and Jewish Thinkers," in Norman Kretzmann and Eleonore Stump, ed., *The Cambridge Companion to Aquinas* (New York: Cambridge University Press, 1993), 60–62.

6. Richard, *La Trinité*, 4, 4, 237–38 (my translation).

7. Richard, *La Trinité*, 2, 12, 131.

8. Chenu, *Nature, Man, and Society*, 233 et passim, citing Richard.

9. Leszek Kolakowski, "The Priest and the Jester," in *Toward a Marxist Humanism: Essays on the Left Today*, trans. J. Z. Peel (New York: Grove Press, 1968), 23–24, says that Personalist philosophers have taken over from theology the notion of mystery, thus mystifying the idea of the person as "non-communicable." He seems to take this to mean "ineffable" or inexpressible in words. While it may well be true that no words suffice to say everything about who an individual person is, the root cause of this ineffability is the uniqueness at the ontological level of each person, and this uniqueness and irreplaceability is the idea conveyed by the medieval term.

10. Richard, *La Trinité*, 3, 25, 221.

11. Ibid.

12. Ibid., 4, 4, 241–43.

13. Ibid., 4, 7, 243–45.

14. Ibid., 4, 10, 249–51.

15. Ibid., 4, 14, 259.

16. Ibid., 4, 16, 263.

17. Ibid., 4, 20, 275.

18. Ibid., 4, 23, 283.

19. Ewert Cousins, "The Notion of the Person in the *De Trinitate* of Richard of Saint Victor," (Ph.D. diss., New York: Fordham University, 1966), 139–44.

20. Cousins, "The Notion of the Person," 155–157.

21. Cousins, "The Notion of the Person," 235–40.

22. See Jean-Pierre Torrell, *Initiation à Saint Thomas d'Aquin: Sa personne et son oeuvre* (Paris: Editions du Cerf, 1993), forthcoming in English translation; James A. Weisheipl, *Friar Thomas d'Aquino: His Life, Thought and Works*, (Washington, DC: The Catholic University of America, 1983); and Kretzmann and Stump, *Cambridge Aquinas*, for extended accounts of Thomas and his work.

23. St. Thomas Aquinas, *Summa Theologiae*, Latin text and English translation (New York: McGraw-Hill Book Company, 1964), 60 vols.; Vol. 6, *The Trinity*, trans. Ceslaus Velecky, I, 29, 3–4 ad 4; further on the notion of person in Thomas, see ibid., III, 16, 12. That the human mind can be used in a laborious way is not surprising; such labor would however be unbecoming for God—as both Thomas and Scotus would have agreed; but Scotus, lacking a theory of analogy of being, would seem to have more difficulty than Thomas in denying human attributes of God. See St. Thomas Aquinas, *On the Power of God*, trans. English Dominican Fathers (London: Burns Oates & Washburn, 1934), q. 9, a. 2, ad 10.

24. Aristotle, *Categories*, 1.

25. 'Person' is predicated analogously of God and creatures. *Summa Theologiae*, I, 29, 4, ad 4.

26. Augustine, *On the Trinity*, V, 5 (6), 179–80.

27. "'Person' in reference to the divine signifies a relation as subsisting."—*Summa Theologiae*, I, 29, 4, c.; 30, 1, c.; 33, 2, ad 1.

28. Thomas Aquinas, *Commentary on the Third Book of Sentences of Peter Lombard* (*Opera Omnia*; [New York: Musurgia Publishers, 1948]), 25 vols., Vol. 7, d. 5, q. 3, a. 2, ad 2 (my translation).

29. Thomas Aquinas, *In 1 Sent.*, Vol. 6, d. 23, q. 1, a. 1, ad 4.

30. *In 1 Sent.*, d. 23, q. 1, a. 1, c.

31. Ibid., d. 23, q. 1, a. 3.

32. "What does not exist substantially [*per se*] is not a person, like an accident, or parts. . . ."—*Summa Theologiae*, I, 29, 1, ad 2, ad 5; q. 75, 4, ad 2. Joseph Owens discusses the importance of the real distinction in "Aristotle and Aquinas," 38–59, in Kretzmann and Stump, ed., *Cambridge Aquinas*. Meister Eckhart, Thomas's fellow-Dominican friar, writing later in the century, emphasizes the oneness of the person: ". . . [some] say that a person is not one, but two people. . . . Such [sensual] people are more properly called animals than persons."—*About Disinterest*, 86–7. "If anything, even to the extent of a hairbreadth, came between the body and the soul, there could be no true union of the two."—*Sermons*, no. 15, 166. "Any person is one. . . ."—*The Defense*, V, 15. ". . . Franz von Baader writes: 'I was often with Hegel in Berlin. Once I read him a passage from Meister Eckhart, who was only a name to him. He was so excited by it that the next day, he read me a whole lecture on Eckhart, which ended with: "There, indeed, we have what we want."' "—R. B. Blakney, *Meister Eckhart: A Modern Translation* (New York: Harper & Row, 1941), Introduction, xiii.

33. Thomas Aquinas, *In I Sent.*, d. 23, q. 1, a. 4, c.

34. See L. W. Geddes and W. A. Wallace, s.v. 'Person', *The New Catholic Encyclopedia*. On the notion of personality in relation to the Incarnation, see Walter Principe, op. cit.

35. "In every created thing, existence and essence, operation and power, differ. . . ."—*Summa Theologiae*, I, Qu. 54, 1, 2, 3, c; 77, 1, c; Qu. 79, 1, c.

36. *Summa Theologiae*, I, Qu. 29, 3, c, ad 2 and 4.

37. Ibid., I, Qu. 29, 4, c.

38. Ibid., I, Qu. 30, 4, c.

39. Ibid., I, Qu. 39, 3, ad 4.
40. Ibid., I, Qu. 29, 3, ad 4.
41. John Duns Scotus, *Opera Omnia* (Vatican City: Typis Polyglottis Vaticana, 1956), Vol. V, *Ordinatio*, I, Dist. 23, Qu. unica, II, 15, 355–57. On the role of the soul and of existence, as well as of place, in the individuation of human beings in Thomas Aquinas, see Kevin White, "Individuation in Aquinas's Super Boethium De Trinitate," *American Catholic Philosophical Quarterly* (hereafter: ACPQ) 69 (1995): 543–56; and, on Scotus's principle of individuation, Timothy B. Noone, "Individuation in Scotus," ACPQ 69 (1995): 527–42.
42. Scotus, *Ordinatio*, ibid., 16, 356.
43. Martin Heidegger, *Being and Time*, trans. J. Macquarrie and E. Robinson (New York: Harper & Row, 1962), I, 3, 93, alludes briefly to the doctrines of analogy and univocity as seen through the eyes of Descartes. Heidegger wrote a thesis on Scotus's doctrine of categories: *Duns Scotus' Theory of the Categories and of Meaning*, trans. Harold Robbins (Ann Arbor, MI: University Microfilms International, 1978). Heribert Mühlen is the author of a study of *Sein und Person nach Johannes Duns Scotus: Beitrag zur Grundlegung einer Metaphysik der Person* (Werl/Westf.: Dietrich-Coelde-Verlag, 1954).
44. Experts differ on ways of explaining Scotus's philosophy. For some of the notions considered here, see John Duns Scotus, *God and Creatures: The Quodlibetal Questions*, trans. Felix Alluntis and Allan B. Wolter (Princeton, NJ: Princeton University Press, 1975), q. 19, a. 3, 428–42 and 535–37; Efrem Bettoni, *Duns Scotus: The Basic Principles of His Philosophy*, trans. B. Bonansea (Westport, CT: Greenwood Press, Publishers, 1979), 60–63, 96–97, and 122–23; and Allan Wolter, *Duns Scotus Philosophical Writings* (London: Thomas Nelson & Sons, 1962), 179: "Briefly, intuition is a simple or nondiscursive knowledge of something *as existing*. Abstract knowledge prescinds from actual existence or non-existence."
45. See Thomas Aquinas, *Summa Theologiae*, I, Qu. 84, 7, c.
46. John Duns Scotus, *Questiones in Librum Primam Sententiarum*, d. 1, q. 1.
47. Scotus, *Ordinatio*, d. 26, Q. unica, (*Opera Omnia*, VI, 51).
48. Scotus, *God and Creatures*, 19.63 (434).
49. See John Duns Scotus, *God and Creatures*, xviii.
50. Thomas Hobbes, *Leviathan* (New York: Collins Books, 1962), Part I, Chap. XVI.
51. Dugald Stewart, *The Collected Works*, (Edinburgh, 1877), I, *Dissertation Exhibiting the Progress of Metaphysical, Ethical, and Political Philosophy Since the Revival of Letters in Europe*, ed. Sir William Hamilton, 2nd. ed. (Edinburgh: T. & T. Clark, 1877), 82.

6

The Vanishing Person:
The *Encyclopaedia Britannica*

I exist in so far as I am a person; and I am a person in so far as I am
conscious.

—*Encyclopaedia Britannica*, Eighth Edition

PERSON: STRUCTURE TO FUNCTION

The *Encyclopaedia Britannica* has been an important cultural force in the English-speaking world since the first edition appeared in 1771.[1] Its founders conceived of it as doing for readers of English something like what the *Encyclopédie*
had done for the French.[2] Its treatment of a question like that of the nature of
the human person at once reflected and influenced the intellectual spirit of its
times. An examination of the *Encyclopaedia*'s definitions of 'person', as well as
related words like 'personality', over the course of its first century or so shows
a tension between the medieval—and ancient—notion of person and an emerging
notion of person that is less structural and more functional than the earlier one.

A principal change in the understanding of the nature of personhood during
this time was that from the person as a substantial entity to that of personhood
as consisting of an act or state of mind, notably that of consciousness.

An examination of its treatment of the word 'person' will therefore provide
an insight into the fate of this word in the last 200 years. Definitions of 'person' as well as related words like 'personality' will be examined.

THE FIRST EDITION

The first edition of the *Encyclopaedia* (1771) defines 'person' as follows:

an individual substance of a rational or intelligent nature. Thus we say, an
ambassador represents the person of his prince; and that, in law, the father
and the son are reputed the same person.[3]

67

A curious feature of this definition is that the examples introduced by the word "thus" do not really seem to illustrate the definition. In Boethius's definition, after which the first sentence in the entry is formed, it is the structure of the person, in a metaphysical sense, that is spelled out. The definition can be logically analyzed in terms of the genus or more general class of beings to which the subject of the definition belongs, namely that of "substance"; this is narrowed by the addition of "individual." "Of a rational nature" indicates that while there are substances of an irrational nature, like trees or dogs, person is not one of these.

The illustration given after "thus," however, does not in any way explain the structure, in this sense, of human personality; rather, it instantiates functions, and especially legal functions, of the person. The second part, beginning "in law," seems directly to contradict the notion of individual substance as Boethius and others understood this notion.

So, to take the first of the two illustrations, the ambassador can indeed be said to represent the person of his prince; but in doing so he does not represent his prince precisely as "an individual substance of a rational or intelligent nature." Rather, the prince is a human person endowed with sovereignty, but his personhood need not be made an explicit object of metaphysical reflection here anymore than when he puts on his crown. Rather, the sense is that when the ambassador acts it is as though the prince were present "in person." The implicit incoherence in the definition invited further reflection and later editions show editors attempting to improve upon the definition with various degrees of success. Before turning to these other editions, we may consider other places in the *Encyclopaedia* in which 'person' and its derivatives appear.

Another entry in the same edition deals with 'personality', as meaning, "in the schools [i.e., for medieval scholastic philosophers and their followers], that which constitutes an individual or distinct person."

There is also another definition of the word in the same work in the article on "metaphysics," although there is no reference to this second definition in the "person" article. This is a Lockean definition, in that it emphasizes personal identity. It reads as follows:

Person stands for an intelligent being, that reasons and reflects, and can consider itself the same thing in different times and places; which it doth by that *consciousness* that is inseparable from thinking. By this every one is to himself what he calls *self*, without considering whether that *self* be continued in the same or divers substances. In this consists *personal identity*, or the sameness of a rational being; and so far as this consciousness extends backward to any past action or thought, so far reaches the identity of that person. It is the same *self* now, it was then: And it is by the same *self*, with this present one that now reflects on it, that that action was done.

Self is that conscious thinking thing, whatever substance it matters not, which is conscious of pleasure or pain, capable of happiness or misery; and so is concerned for itself as far as that consciousness extends. That with which the consciousness of this present thinking thing can join itself, makes the same person, and is one self with it; and so attributes to itself and owns all the actions of that thing as its own, as far as that consciousness reaches.

This *personal identity* is the object of reward and punishment, being that by which every one is concerned for himself. If the *consciousness* went along with the little finger, when that was cut off, it would be the same self that was just before concerned for the whole body.

If the same *Socrates*, waking and sleeping, did not partake of the same consciousness, they would not be the same *person*. . . .

But suppose I wholly lose the memory of some parts of my life . . . so that I shall never be conscious of them again: Am I not the *same person* that did those actions . . . .? I answer, that we must here take notice what the word *I* is applied to, which in this case is the man only: And the same man being presumed to be the same person, *I* is easily here supposed to stand also for the same person. But if it be possible for the same man to have distinct incommunicable consciousness at different times, it is past doubt the same man would, at different times, make different persons. Which we see is the sense of mankind in the solemnest declaration of their opinions, human law not punishing the mad man for the sober man's actions, nor the sober man for what the mad man did; thereby making them two persons.[4]

Human laws may in fact punish the sleepwalker and/or the drunken person for the actions they perform, when it is impossible to be sure that they did not in fact have sufficient consciousness to realize what they were doing.

It is clear that these two definitions of person, the one standing alone and the other embedded in the article on metaphysics, tend in different directions. One employed the ancient Boethian definition, though without much understanding; the other attempted to argue from forensic usage to a definition of 'person' appropriate in legal situations. They were both to undergo various transformations in succeeding editions.

SECOND EDITION

The second edition, of 1781, carries the definition of 'person' found in the first, except that the word 'or' between 'rational' and 'intelligent' is dropped.

First Edition	Second Edition
an individual substance	an individual substance
of a rational or	of a rational intelligent
intelligent nature	nature

The second edition also contained a slight but important change in the definition of 'personality'. The earlier definition found 'personality' to be "that which constitutes an individual a distinct person." The newer definition replaces the word 'a' with 'or', thus bringing about a significant change in meaning from the first edition:

First Edition	Second Edition
that which constitutes an individual a distinct person	that which constitutes an individual or distinct person

The word "individual" in the earlier edition can be seen to function as an adjective, equivalent to "distinct." In the newer definition it seems rather to function as a substantive, so that thanks to personality, this individual becomes a person.

THIRD EDITION

The Preface to the third edition (1797), explaining the overall purpose of the work, says:

> In ancient Greece, where philosophy first assumed a systematic form, all the objects of human thought were ranged under ten categories or predicaments; and every thing which could be affirmed or denied of these categories was supposed to be comprehended under five classes called predicables. . . . To this ancient arrangement of human knowledge many insuperable objections have been urged. But it must be confessed, that the arrangements which have been proposed in its stead, by the sages of modern times, have little claim to greater perfection. . . .
> Locke says expressly, that as the objects of our knowledge are confined to *substances, modes,* and *ideas,* so we can discover nothing of these, but *1st,* their *identity* or *diversity, 2nd,* their *relation; 3rd,* their *co-existence* or *necessary connection;* and, *4th,* their *real existence.* . . .[5]

The editor is evidently well acquainted with the difficulty presented by the two definitions of 'person' in this third edition, and with their underlying Aristotelian and Lockean assumptions, respectively. Under the editorship of Dr. George Gleig (who had previously corresponded with the first editor, Colin Macfarquhar), the entry on 'person' was considerably expanded from that of the second—from the few lines of the second edition to an entire column. To the definition as given in the second edition two paragraphs were added; the first dealt with etymology and the other with the meaning of 'individual'.

The first paragraph explains that the meaning of 'person' comes from "impersonating" or counterfeiting, and that the word originally referred to an actor's mask, in which "sound rolls around"; then

> other people [besides masked characters in plays], who were at the same time distinguished by something in their form, character, &c. whereby they

might be known, came likewise to be called by the Latins *personae* and by the Greeks *prosopa*. Again, as actors rarely represented any but great and illustrious characters, the word came at length to import the mind, as being that whose dispositions constitute the character.... Things merely corporeal, as a stone, a plant, or a horse, were called *hypostases* or *supposita*, but never *persons*. Hence the learned suppose, that the same name *person* came to be used to signify some dignity....

The second paragraph considers 'individual' as logically indivisible because it cannot be predicated of another and as physically individual because (1) "the person is the whole principle of acting" and (2)

negatively, as when we say, with the Thomists, &c. that a person consists in this, that it does not exist in another as a more perfect being. Thus a man, though he consists of two different things, *viz.* body and spirit, is not two persons; because neither part of itself is a complete principle of action, but one person, since the manner of his consisting of body and spirit is such as constitutes one whole principle of action; nor does he exist in any other as a more perfect being; as, for example, Socrates's foot does in Socrates....

The definition of the word 'personality' in this third edition differs from that of the second only in the addition of the word 'is': "is that which constitutes...."

Finally, the third edition refers one to the article on metaphysics for a treatment of "personal identity." In this article, running to ten columns (in contrast to one and a half in the first edition), the theologian Bishop Joseph Butler's refutation of Locke's account of personal identity is given, with objections of a philosopher, Mr. Cooper. To Bishop Butler,

Mr. Locke's observations upon this subject appear hasty; ... But some of those hasty observations have been carried to a strange length by others; whose notion ... amounts ... to this: "That personality is not a permanent but a transient thing; That it lives and dies, begins and ends, continually: ... That our substance is indeed continually changing: but ... it is not substance, but consciousness alone, which constitutes personality; which consciousness, being successive, cannot be the same in any two moments, nor consequently the personality constituted by it."[6]

The author of the article counters that "it is only that which thinks and wills that any man considers, in this case, his person; ..." He makes his meaning more explicit later:

if there be united to the brain an immaterial being, which is the subject of sensation, consciousness, and will, &c. it is obvious, that all the *intellectual powers* which properly constitute the person, must be inherent in that being.

Here it may be noted that the medieval "faculty psychology," as it is sometimes called, distinguished between acts (of seeing, for example) and powers (like that of sight). The latter must be in working order, as it were, for acts to occur when they do. The acts are intermittent, the powers enduring. Neither act nor power, however, is identical with the substantially existing individual who sees, who is the ultimate agent of the act, and who uses the power he or she possesses. The author of the article in this third edition makes a different claim: that the person not only uses her powers but is constituted a person by them.

If it is the *powers* of thinking and willing that constitute the person, there is no need to reflect upon whether there is a change in a *substance* to be taken into account in considering identity of persons.[7] It is clear that 'substance' here does not mean what it meant for either Aristotle or Thomas Aquinas. Here it is a Lockean "unknown substrate" that is in question.

SUCCEEDING EDITIONS

The fourth edition (1810), edited by Dr. James Millar, was intended to bring about greater unity of thought and expression than the third had achieved under two different editors. The preface attributes to a Prof. Robison and Dr. Gleig the responsibility for the philosophical articles. These are copied almost word for word from the third edition.

The fifth edition contained no material changes from the fourth. The sixth (1824) added supplementary volumes to bring up to date the material in the two earlier editions. Dugald Stewart's observations on the history of philosophy, and Aristotle in particular, are included in one supplementary volume. He notes that Martin Luther hated Aristotle, and that Reformation leaders, with the exception of Melancthon, also turned away from Aristotle's doctrines.[8]

About substance, Stewart remarks in a note:

I employ the scholastic word *substance*, . . . but I am fully aware of the strong objections to which it is liable, not only as a wide deviation from popular use, which has appropriated it to things material and tangible, but as implying a great . . . degree of positive knowledge. . . .[9]

Stewart observes about the Aristotelian categories:

In consequence of the stress laid on the *predicaments*, men became accustomed in their youth to imagine, that, in order to know the nature of anything, it was sufficient to know under what *predicament* or *category* it ought to be arranged; . . .[10]

THE SEVENTH EDITION

The seventh edition (1842), edited by Macvey Napier, carries the same article on personal identity as did the third. The editor remarks in the Preface that he had at first "resolved to have" the article on metaphysics "examined anew, . . .

under the more appropriate title of the Philosophy of Mind," principally because "it does nothing like justice to that Metaphysical School native to Scot-
land, and distinguished by the names of Reid and Stewart," so much appreciated
abroad but little at home. In view of the existence of Stewart's Dissertation,
however, he dropped the idea.

The article on person in the seventh edition surprisingly drops the word
'substance' entirely: "PERSON, an individual of a rational and intelligent nature. Thus we say, an ambassador. . . ."

EIGHTH AND NINTH EDITIONS

In the eighth edition (1859) the 'person' entry is new. Any reference to the
Greek root of the word (with its bodily connotations) or to the Boethian definition is omitted:

> PERSON, PERSONALITY. The word *person* (Latin *persona*, "a mask," de-
> rived, according to Gabius Bassus, in Aulus Gellius, V. 7, from *persono*, "to
> sound through"), from being originally applied to a player's mask, came to
> signify the individual wearing it. Again, as one individual is distinguished
> from another more by the internal character than by the external traits of
> his nature, the term suffered a further transference of meaning, in being
> used in a sense synonymous with *man*, who is an intelligent, free, and re-
> sponsible being. Person in this sense is distinguished from *thing*. Deity, con-
> sidered as a creative cause and governing intelligence distinct from the universe
> is a *person*. *Personality* is the idea of a person carried to its highest degree of
> generality. The essence of personality is generally supposed by philosophers
> to reside in the will.[11]

This edition could have been available to the youthful John Dewey. If so, it
would have reinforced an impression of the mental character of human personality.

The article on metaphysics in this edition is no longer based on a Lockean
model but has rather a Kantian flavor.[12] This article also appeals to members
of the Scottish School like Hamilton, Reid, and Stewart, as well as to Descartes[13]
and Leibniz. The section entitled "of the consciousness of personality" in the
eighth edition includes the following:

> The notion of a state of consciousness, with no one to be conscious of it, is
> as absurd as the opposite fiction of a conscious self with nothing to be con-
> scious of. If the latter has given rise to the extravagances of rational psychol-
> ogy, the former is the basis of a not less extravagant reaction, which in its
> logical consequences leads to the consistent denial of personality, of free-
> dom, of responsibility; nay, of the very conceptions of substance and cause,
> the foundations of all philosophy.[14]

Without presuming to judge the purveyors of an extravagant rational psychology, one may note that the Aristotelian doctrine of the various powers is

based not upon "a conscious self with nothing to be conscious of," but upon observation and inference. From the observed fact that a dog responds to a command, one may justifiably conclude to the existence in the dog of a power to respond to what is heard, and to a power of hearing that accounts for an act of hearing. Similarly one may conclude to the existence of other powers from observing acts. But this sort of observation does not support a monadic "conscious self."

Another section, "Of the Real in Psychology," states that:

> My own consciousness is not merely the test of my real existence, but it actually constitutes it. I exist in so far as I am a person; and I am a person in so far as I am conscious. . . . My consciousness does not *prove* my existence, because it *is* my existence. . . . The opinion of Locke, that the soul does not always think, is tenable only as a part of that false psychology which regards the soul as a substance projected, as it were, out of consciousness, the unknown substratum imagined as the support of known accidents. The unconscious substratum of possible ideas may be a *soul* in some arbitrary and unmeaning definition of that term; but assuredly it is not *myself*. . . . In so far as the rudiments of my body existed prior to the birth of consciousness, in so far they were not parts of myself: and I, as a person, had no existence.[15]

Our bodies undergo constant change in the particles that constitute them, "Yet amidst all these changes, the conscious subject, the personal self, continues one and unchanged."[16] Without the essential conditions of consciousness, time and free agency, however, I could not exist as a person: "Succession in time is thus manifested as a constituent element of my personal existence, without which I could not be conscious of that existence; and, as consciousness is in this case reality, without which *I* could not exist." Again, "Volition is not, indeed, the whole of personality, but it is one necessary element of it; . . ."

Time, which Aristotle considered to be the "measure of motion according to before and after," and thus dependent upon movement in the material world, is here considered as "a constituent element of my personal existence," needed for consciousness. How time thus constitutes the consciousness that is constitutive of personality is not clear. What is evident is that the person is here reduced to a function, an act—that of consciousness (or perhaps, the power to be conscious, or the state of consciousness). In the Boethian definition the person was the actor, the doer, the substantial being capable of acts. The new definition eliminates the substance in favor of what Aristotle would have called accidents of the substance, its actions.

While the treatment of the person in the eighth edition's article on metaphysics is different from that of the preceding editions, it is at one with them in its conviction that the person is the mind, and the conscious mind at that.

By the ninth edition (1885), the article on 'person' is dropped entirely, (though in other articles it contains allusions to many of the notions mentioned above).

CONCLUSION

It is evident that in the period 1771–1859 the notion of the nature of personhood was the object of earnest consideration in the English-speaking intellectual world. During this time the understanding of the notion of personhood changed from that of a substantial existent (based on Aristotle's "substance") to that of an act or state of mind, notably that of consciousness (what Aristotle would have called an "accident").

The elimination of the article on "person" from the ninth edition of the *Encyclopaedia* is perhaps to be understood as either an expression of exasperation with the confused state of the discussion of this topic or else as a decision as to the diminished importance of this question in the newly emerging psychology. In either case it goes a long way toward explaining the "state of the question" at the end of the nineteenth century. Dewey may have made use of the eighth edition's definition; Trendelenburg's notes on this subject, possibly made available to him through his early mentor, George Morris, may also have been known to him. In any case, neither the *Encyclopaedia* nor Trendelenburg's notes provide reliable access to the ancient/medieval notion of person.

A principal change in the understanding of the nature of personhood during this time was that from the person as a substantial entity, modelled on the notion of Aristotle's category of substance, to that of personhood as consisting of an act or state of mind, notably that of consciousness—what Aristotle would have considered an accident.

It is against this historical background that the notion of person needs to be considered today. Probably a majority of present-day discussions of the nature of human personhood take their point of departure from the Kantian postulation of the need for persons to be responsible morally (in order to make sense of the necessary existence of the moral law). In their mode of procedure, furthermore, they tend to assume a Cartesian dichotomy between mind and matter, effectively precluding reference to the ancient and medieval notions of the human person as a unitary, yet essentially composite, being.

Part 3 of this work considers what might constitute an explanation of the nature of human personhood from the perspective of the ancient and medieval tradition.

NOTES

1. Harvard President Eliot's copy of James Baldwin, *A Guide to Systematic Readings in the Encyclopaedia Britannica* (New York: The Werner Company, 1897) contains pencil marks in its table of contents on three chapters dealing with world literature, perhaps a source for his Harvard Classics.

2. See James Lough, *The Encyclopédie in Eighteenth-Century England and Other Studies* (Newcastle upon Tyne: Oriel Press, 1970), 23.

3. *Encyclopaedia Britannica; or A Dictionary of Arts and Sciences . . . in the order of the Alphabet* (Edinburgh: A. Bell and C. Macfarquhar, 1771; hereafter: EB), 1st ed., Vol. III, 469. The next entry reads as follows: "Person, in grammar, a term applied to such nouns or pronouns, as, being either prefixed or understood, are the nominatives in all the inflections of a verb; or it is the agent or patient in all finite and personal verbs."

4. EB, 1st ed., s.v. "Metaphysics."

5. EB, 3rd ed., vi. In the same preface it is made clear that the third edition had two editors, Colin Macfarquhar for the first twelve volumes up to "Mysteries," and Dr. George Gleig for the last six. It was Dr. Gleig (a "formidable scholar, specializing in the moral and physical sciences," according to Herman Kogan, *The Great EB* [Chicago: The University of Chicago Press, 1958], 23) who wrote the article on "Metaphysics" for the 3rd edition.

6. For a discussion of Butler and Reid, see C. McCall, *Concepts of Person*, Chap. 14.

7. EB, 3rd ed., "Metaphysics."

8. Preface to the First Dissertation, 23: "Luther, who was perfectly aware of the corruptions which the Romish church had contrived to connect with their veneration for the Stagirite [Aristotle], not only threw off the yoke himself, but . . . speaks of Aristotle with most unbecoming asperity and contempt." And, ". . . Melanchthon had . . . unfortunately given the sanction of his name to the doctrines of the Peripatetic [Aristotelian] school: but still, among the Reformers in general, the credit of these doctrines gradually declined, and a spirit of research and of improvement prevailed." In a note, Stewart adds: "'he [Luther] hated Aristotle, but highly esteemed Cicero, as a wise and good man.'" It is interesting that the name of Cicero comes up repeatedly as an example in reference to treatments of the nature of 'person'.

9. Ibid., 88.

10. Ibid., 160, n. I.

11. On the importance of will and choice for human action, see Alan Donagan, *Choice: The Essential Element in Human Action* (New York: Routledge and Kegan Paul, 1987), especially 42, 155–56, and 167–68.

12. Immanuel Kant, a century after Locke, saw the need to bring the person back to the center of his own philosophy. Kant had been sceptical of the validity of human knowledge in the speculative realm. But the very doubtfulness of the results of speculation seemed to call for the act of a person—moral action—to assure what could be achieved in no other way, a knowledge of God.

13. Descartes, unlike Hobbes and Locke, had little to say about personhood. For him the mind—"thinking thing"—a quasi-substance, along with another quasi-substance, "extended thing"—roughly, the body—made the uneasy unity of oneself. (See, however, his letter to Princess Elizabeth of June, 1643, cited in G. N. A. Vesey, *The Embodied Mind* [London: George Allen and Unwin, 1965], 11, note 1: "that notion of their union which everybody always has in himself without doing philosophy—viz., that there is one single person who has at once body and consciousness. . . .") Inasmuch as Descartes did not concern himself with personhood as such, he stands outside the scope of this discussion. But his influence persists in the fascination of modern thinkers with the mind and with "Philosophy of Mind" rather than with Aristotle's "Psychology" (or science of the *soul*—the principle of life in the body—) that endures to the present time.

14. EB, 8th ed., "Metaphysics."

15. EB, 8th ed., "Metaphysics." Cf. Ludwig Feuerbach, "Against the Dualism of Body and Soul," cited in Franz Grégoire, *Aux Sources de la pensée de Marx* (Louvain: Institut Supérieur de Philosophie, 1947), 340: "Neither [does] the soul think and experience—for the soul is only the personified, hypostatized function or appearance of thinking, experiencing and willing, turned into a being—nor [does] the brain. . . ." (my translation.)

16. EB, 8th ed., "Metaphysics."

PART 3

An Onto-Logical Account of the Person

Aristotle's substance is not an 'underlying somewhat', a 'something-I-know-not-what', a queer entity inferred 'behind' or 'beneath' the appearances or characteristics, a residue discovered by the process of 'stripping off' as Descartes discovered the 'substance' of wax, or a postulated and unseen thing-in-itself behind the veil of phenomena.

—Michael Novak

Part 3 aims to demonstrate some of the ways in which an understanding of the categories can illuminate one's understanding of human personhood. An initial chapter deals with substance as the fundamental category for understanding person, particularly with reference to its historical settings.

The remaining chapters deal with personhood as it can be grasped through the various accidental categories, especially those of quality, relation, and action.

7

An Individual Substance

Every substance is thought to indicate a *this*.

—Aristotle

SUBSTANCE AND ITS BAD PRESS

Substance has no doubt suffered from a bad reputation in recent centuries. Some of the historical reasons for this have been discussed in Chapter 6.[1] An additional reason might be the tendency to confuse the doctrines of the ancient philosophers Plato and Aristotle. A recent writer finds that Aristotle's analysis of a proposition into subject, predicate, and a form of "to be" leads to the

> twin errors of supposing that there are universals—e.g., redness— in some way existing or subsisting apart from red objects, and of supposing that there is a fabulous 'substance' existing apart from the qualities which it possesses.[2]

It was precisely to avoid problems raised by Plato's "subsisting redness," however, that Aristotle insisted upon the individual tangible man or horse as examples of his substance.[3]

It is true that substance, being the ultimate or highest genus of things classified in the categories, enters into the definition of all the others in some way or other. This makes it hard to talk about, because whatever words one uses to describe it themselves presuppose it. We shall, nevertheless, try here to say something about it in reference to the human person. The word 'substance' in English comes from Latin words meaning to "stand under." As such, it probably does not do justice to Aristotle's Greek *ousia*, which refers to being.

SUBSTANCE: DEFINITION AND FUNCTIONS

The *Oxford English Dictionary* defines substance in a philosophical sense as "a being that subsists by itself; a separate or distinct thing; hence, gen., a thing, a being." The first part of the definition—in using the phrase "by itself"—might

80

be taken (as Descartes seems to have done) to refer to God alone. But "a separate or distinct thing" precludes this misunderstanding. And "a thing, a being" fits well with Aristotle's examples of this man and this horse. Evidently "by itself" is to be taken to refer to a being that can perdure, persist in existence in a way in which some other being—an accident—cannot (although it is evidently possible for the height of the person who has just died to continue to exist in the now dead body). The point is not so much temporal as ontological: how long the person or the person's height continues to exist is beside the principal point, which concerns the *way* of existing of the substance as contrasted with that of the accident.

Substance functions, in the realm of physical theorizing, as an economical hypothesis: physical substances—unlike purely mathematical entities, like the number 3, for example—have characteristics like resistance that significantly limit the kind of activity they can receive or perform. Many Western philosophers have been reluctant, since the time of Plato, to sever their ties with mathematics. Mathematically trained philosophers like Whitehead tend to see philosophy as a branch of mathematics. He regards the atom of time, the instant, as the most real and creative entity in his universe, rather than as the mere limiting point on a continuum of time that it is for Aristotle. For Aristotle, it is the physical world of individual substances that lies at the basis of natural science. The importance of the point in question can be seen in an example: manipulating genetic material both brings about something new and at the same time is limited by the given material. For Aristotle, it is the living whole, the fruit fly, for example, rather than the part, the chromosome, that is the substance. The shape of the chromosome is not the substance; the fruit fly is.

Working in a climate of opinion established by Plato, Aristotle refuted by various arguments Plato's theory of Ideas as explanatory realities. Whereas Plato spoke of an Idea that would be imitated by an earthly counterpart, Aristotle argues, against this view, that it would lead to an endless series of intervening entities: would not a third man, and a fourth, and so on, be needed to explain how this man is related to the Ideal Man of Plato? Since Plato's theory was worked out in the context of questions about scientific knowledge, Aristotle needed to address the same questions and answer them better than his teacher had done.

When one looks at substance from a metaphysical point of view, the "problem of universals" arises, a problem solved differently by Plato and Aristole. "Second" substance is the name Aristotle gives to the universal such as humanity, and for him, unlike Plato, it is indeed second to the really existing individual.

In neither Hindu nor Confucian thought do the words 'science', 'substance', and 'person' appear together. Aristotle lived after the earliest Hindu sacred books were written, but even if his works had been available to the writers of those books, it is unlikely that Aristotle's notion of substance would have taken hold in a culture in which the fundamental sameness and eternal recurrence of things were the dominant notions. Confucian thinkers subordinated theoretical questions about nature to practical issues important to social life.

A common objection to substance is that it does not allow for a relational view of the person. Such an objection mistakes what Aristotle means by substance. For Aristotle, the accident of relation itself depends upon substance, logically and ontologically. Logically, to speak of relation depends on the notion of substance. And, for something to be related, it must be. Thus, substance is the foundation of relation, in that it underlies the accident of relation itself. When substance is understood in this sense, the force of the objection vanishes.

Consideration of an example taken from Aristotle's study of friendship may help here. This study, concerning the nature and kinds of friendship, is found in the *Nicomachean Ethics*, Books 8 and 9, and it is one of the most interesting in Aristotle. Friends regard one another as other selves, and, depending upon the basis for their appreciation of one another, they are said to be pleasant, useful, or simply good to one another. If the two friends be thought of as "individual substances," it is at once evident that these substances are not unrelated.

To be sure, little can be said about substance. Like the puppeteer whose hands and voice are essential to the action and speech of the puppets, substance is veiled behind the appearances despite being essential to the operation. Whatever is of interest in things seems to belong to the accidents, or even the objects toward which the accidental knowing powers are directed—not the substantial knowing subject.

Despite its lack of philosophical glamor, however, substantial existence is essential to the real operation of things and persons in the world. Much of the dissatisfaction expressed by recent philosophers, in reference to substance, seems to have been directed toward a caricature, a stereotype that has little to do with what Aristotle had in mind when he talked about *ousia*.[4] Substance can be seen either as the ultimate existing thing, or as the ability to exist of such ultimate existing things as "this man, this horse." To deny either that substance exists or that there is such a thing as substantial reality is to make a statement impossible to prove. Sometimes the denial of substance is made as part of a denial of metaphysics as a discipline. But to deny metaphysics, as Aristotle observed, is to make a metaphysical statement.

It is the Lockean "unknown substrate" that should be repudiated by those who decry substance as useless, rather than the Aristotelian substance. Locke's substance does no work; Aristotle's was invented to defend the reality of change and of science dealing with change against both Parmenides, who denied change, and Heraclitus, for whom change was evidence against the possibility of knowledge.[5]

Since substance is understood correlatively with accidents, it is through a grasp of accidental being that one is able to come to a knowledge of substance. Thus when I see a leaf change color, I may realize that since the leaf persists through its change in color, it is distinct from whatever color it has at a given time. Similarly, though the size and shape of the leaf may change over time, the leaf remains identifiably the same.

Although some "accidents" like color and shape are able to be seen, however, and substance is not, it is possible to argue to the reality of substance on the basis of accidental existence: because accidents (by definition) exist in substances but cannot exist alone, something is required that does exist by itself, *per se* or *in se*. If this is true, then it would seem that one might choose from among the following options:

1. One might choose to ignore the question of the manner of existence entirely, thus losing an important tool for explaining change, for example.
2. One might decide to regard everything as a substantial existent, the color in the rose as much as the rose itself, which flies in the face of experience: we do see changes taking place in aspects of things which do not change the things themselves directly.
3. One might see everything as purely accidental in existence, with the irrationality of an infinite regress: accident 1 would exist in accident 2, and so on, indefinitely.
4. Finally, there is the option Aristotle adopted, that of distinguishing between those realities that exist in themselves, substances, and those able to exist only in another, accidents.

It may indeed be difficult to say much about substance, but the worse error lies in denying it, rather than in failing to say much about it. The mistake of taking everything or nothing for a substance or of simply ignoring the issue is probably worse than that which might be involved in giving it serious consideration.

How then does Aristotle define 'substance'? He gives its most fundamental sense in the *Categories* when he says that a

> substance, spoken of in the most fundamental, primary, and highest sense of the word is that which is neither said of a subject nor present in a subject; e.g., an individual man or an individual horse.[6]

Much discussion has centered upon this definition and upon other references to the meaning of 'substance' throughout Aristotle's works.[7] For the purpose of the present work, however, there is no need to enter into a more detailed treatment of the history of this discussion. Our concern is with the meaning of substance as it relates to the notion of person and contributes to clarifying the related aspects of subsistence, agency, and soul.

ARISTOTLE'S SUBSTANCE AND 'PERSON' IN BOETHIUS

It seems clear that Boethius relies on the fundamental meaning of 'substance' as defined in Aristotle's *Categories* when he makes 'substance' the genus of his own definition of person. In this famous and historically important text, which we have discussed in Chapter 4, Boethius defines 'person' as an "individual *substance* of a rational nature."[8]

Boethius uses a logical method of elimination to arrive at his definition of 'person'. In this way he makes his reader realize that the person must be a substance by pointing out that a person could not be something inhering in another being, that is, an "accident" of a substance, nor could a person be a mere logical entity, a "second substance," like "humanity."

SUBSTANCE AND SUBSISTENCE

A horse can be encountered in nature. It can be seen and heard, its image can be recalled at will by normal persons. What cannot be encountered is its substantiality as such, its state of being able to exist in itself. In the case of the notion of substantiality, the mind has creatively intervened to set up criteria for belonging to the class of things called "substances." Nothing in the natural world precisely corresponds to this notion; it is founded nonetheless upon realities in the world, with the particular aspect of a thing's being able to exist in itself emphasized. Thus, although substance is not like a peach, a thing in the natural world, substantiality is, Aristotle would say, that which makes the peach able to exist as a thing in itself. To "subsist" is to do what a substance does, to exist in itself.[9] "Accidents" thus lack subsistence.

SUBSTANCE AND AGENCY

If the person is the ultimately important reality in creation, a person must be the actor, the one able to assume responsibility for acts, which only something with the characteristics of a "first substance," that is, the individual, can be.[10]

The accident, inherent in a substance, cannot initiate action. It is the substantial, existing being alone—the horse, the man—not the color of either, that runs. But, of course, the inherent accidents clearly share in the activity of the being: when the horse runs, it does not leave its color behind.

Similarly, the logical subject or second substance, ("mankind" for example), is not able to act in the real world, being a product only of someone's mind; and persons are eminently real. The principal characteristic of substantiality is that of independent existence in the real world. But independence does not involve some sort of Leibnizian monad unrelated to any other being. Rather, Aristotle accepts the existence and relatedness of the bodies encountered in the world.

THE SOUL: A PERSON?

In Boethius's world, the definition of 'person' needed to be applicable to the divine, as well as to human persons. Thus, he seems to have in mind a kind of generic definition of person, one that will apply to persons both with and without bodies. As such, it seems to emphasize the spiritual aspect of personality, and this unstated emphasis persists until the time of Locke.

Does the human soul, which Aristotle saw as the "form" of the matter constituting the body, qualify as an individual substance? It has been argued (for example, by Plato, in the *Phaedo*) that it does: It is able to subsist, that is to say, to exist in its own right; it can maintain its existence even after the loss of the body. The reason for affirming this is that the human soul has an operation, thinking, which is to some extent independent of the body.

But to say that thinking is independent of the body is not to maintain that the soul, considered as the animating principle of the human body, can come to know things in the first instance apart from the body. According to Aristotle, human knowledge is acquired by coming into contact with things through our bodily senses, seeing them, for example. It involves, furthermore, accepting them into a mental sphere where they can be preserved as images and memories even when not physically present. This mental sphere seems to be common to both human beings and the higher animals (or, to all living things, some theorists would say). What dogs and dolphins seem to lack, however, is access to a spiritual world, a world of understanding in which ideas like that of substance, derived ultimately from the world through the outer and inner senses, can be dealt with in themselves, apart from their moorings to material things. If it is indeed possible for an "accidental" thought to be entertained without direct reference to the body, then it would seem to be necessary for it to exist in a spiritual substance.

Is the human soul, then, a spiritual substance? It is a distinct existing spiritual being, Thomas Aquinas holds, but not a complete substance. It is complete from the point of view of subsistence, of being able to exist by itself (unlike an accidental being). But from the point of view of performing distinctively human acts, it is incomplete, since by definition a soul animates a body, and it is the living, embodied being that acts. And, with reference to the question of what a person is, since a person is by definition a complete being, the soul as such is not a person.

SUBSTANCE, NATURE, ESSENCE

'Substance' was for Aristotle a kind of ultimate reference point in the sciences of logic, of metaphysics, and of physics. The meaning of the word remained identifiably the same throughout the works, yet it took on a distinctive coloring, as it were, in the different environments in which it was used. Metaphysics, for example, considers subtleties about substance that physics need not, since physics deals, not with all things, but only with things that change—things in the natural world. In this world, 'nature' does not ordinarily refer to the substance itself as such but rather to the source of its activity, as a kind of component: substance is what one is, nature what one has.[11]

Thomas Aquinas's great contribution to philosophy lay in the emphasis he placed upon the real distinction between essence—what a thing is—and existence—the fact that it is. The distinction functions throughout his philosophy, making it clear that anything created exists thanks to the divine gift of existence to that creature, during each moment of its continued being. And for him, substance lies not on the side of existence, but rather on that of the aptitude for existing, the potentiality for existing in or by itself (*esse in se* or *per se*). To arrive at this conclusion, however, requires a good deal of reasoning.

John Duns Scotus prefers to call the person an "existence" rather than a "substance," because while "existence" implies standing—as does "substance"—"existence" seems to say "standing out from" rather than "standing under." And so it makes immediately explicit the distinctness that the complete being has (and thus, the impossibility of a "partial substance" or "incomplete substance"—like the soul—being a person). The person thus understood is immediately seen as a being that is related to that from which or whom he or she "stands out."[12]

These are the sorts of considerations that underlie the different definitions of 'person' that held sway in the Middle Ages. Constrained both by the demands of Aristotelian and Augustinian usage and also by the requirements of the dogmas of faith in the Incarnation (which holds that one Person has two natures) and the Trinity (that one God is in three Persons), the great doctors fashioned their definitions in such a way as to be able to make consistent and adequate statements about the things they encountered in the world around them so that these could be discussed in scientific terms.

All of them agree, in general, in their view of what it means to be a person, for example on the point that the human person is a composite of body and spiritual soul, with no possibility of just a soul, or just a body, being a human person. It is possible for other sorts of beings, like angels, to exist, with or without matter. But a human being could not be a human person in the ordinary, complete sense without being embodied.

The words 'substance', 'nature', and 'essence' are thus sometimes used to mean the same reality, although clearly from different points of view: essence from the point of view of definition, nature from that of source of characteristic activity (it is natural for fish to swim and birds to fly), and substance from that of aptness to exist by itself. These questions will be explored further in the following chapter.

CONCLUSION

From the unproblematic "this man, this horse" to the Byzantine intricacies of subsistence and immortality is a long journey that required volumes of explanation and proof for Aristotle and for those medieval philosophers who followed him. Physics, logic, and metaphysics make their respective contributions to the notion of substance as it was used by Aristotle.

It is understandable that Aristotle's philosophy is in some respects outdated, and that the ordinary person today finds no more compelling need to return to his great sketch of the universe than to understand quarks as ultimate building blocks of material things. An ignorant denial of either, however, ill befits those whose lives may be impacted by the principles in question. Thus, it is the purpose of these chapters to show how an understanding of the nature of human personality may be enhanced by a knowledge of its history.

NOTES

1. Kenneth Barber explains succinctly the epistemological reasons for the disfavor into which 'substance' fell in modern times, especially after Descartes. See Kenneth F. Barber's introduction in Kenneth F. Barber and Jorge J. E. Gracia, eds., *Individuation and Identity in Early Modern Philosophy* (Albany: State University of New York Press, 1994), 1–11.

2. E. R. Emmet, *Learning to Philosophize* (Baltimore, MD: Penguin Books, 1968), 48.

3. See Jorge J. E. Gracia, *Individuality: An Essay on the Foundations of Metaphysics* (Albany: The State University of New York Press, 1988). He discusses the views of philosophers, throughout the ages, about individuality, for example: "Duns Scotus . . . speaks of natures as having being and unity. . . . And to individuality he grants the status of a formality which he called . . . the 'thisness' of the individual" (120).

4. Max Scheler both affirms and denies substance. See John H. Nota, *Max Scheler: The Man and His Work*, trans. Theodore Plantinga and John H. Nota (Chicago, IL: Franciscan Herald Press, 1983). Scheler speaks of "act-substance," evidently trying to express an active rather than an inert notion of substance. Perhaps he is trying to get to a more "energetic" view of substance, than is generally held today, in which case he would be approaching Aristotle's *ousia*. Karol Wojtyla, in his early work, criticizes Scheler for his repudiation of substance, at the same time as he apparently borrows many of Scheler's themes for his own "act-person."

5. See Aristotle *Physics* 1.2.185b20–3.187a10.

6. Aristotle *Categories* 5.2a11–14; see also 5.3b10 in *Aristotle's Categories and Propositions*, trans. Hippocrates G. Apostle (Grinnell, IA: The Peripatetic Press, 1980).

7. No attempt is made here to give a complete account of the notion of substance. We intend only to review and legitimate some areas of discussion where these touch upon the notion of the human person. See M. L. O'Hara, ed., *Substances and Things*, for recent essays on the problems surrounding this fundamental Aristotelian notion. Parts of the present chapter are adapted from the introduction to this work.

8. Boethius, *Against Eutyches*, II–III.

9. Thomas de Vio Cardinal Cajetan (1469–1534), a Thomist writer, sees "rational subsistence" or "subsistence in a rational nature" as the proper definition of 'person'. Subsistence, in his view, is a mode of substance which completes individual nature, making it complete and unassumable by another person—that is, "incommunicable"—and ordered to its own existence.

10. Troels Engberg-Pedersen, "Stoic Philosophy and the Concept of the Person," in *The Person and the Human Mind: Issues in Ancient and Modern Philosophy*, ed. Christopher Gill (Oxford: Clarendon Press, 1990), 109–135, argues that the notion of individual in the Boethian definition can be traced to Stoic sources, and that the Stoics addressed questions similar to those of Kant regarding the relation between an objective, universal norm of morality and the engaged moral human being with his own unique perspective.

11. Aristotle *Physics* 1.7.191a11; 2.l.192b33–35.

12. Robert A. Connor, "Relational *Esse* and the Person," *The American Catholic Philosophical Association Proceedings*, (1991) 65: 253–267, argues for making existence (*esse*) rather than substance the fundamental note of "person" in a Thomistic theological framework.

8

Quality and the Rational Nature

Confucius never discussed strange phenomena, physical exploits, disorder, or spiritual beings.

—Analects

NATURE: AN ANALOGOUS TERM

The preceding chapter has shown that the person is properly described as a substantial being, an "individual substance." The remainder of Boethius's definition, "of a rational nature," narrows the field of those to whom the definition is applicable. Not every individual substance, but only those able to reason, or having intellectual powers, can be called persons.

To understand what is entailed by the expression, "of a rational nature," the meaning of 'natural', and of 'rational'—or 'intellectual'—powers, must be examined. This chapter considers these terms as Aristotle generally uses them.

'Nature' is a word with meanings that have connoted different things in different ages. In earlier eras it might have been thought of as opposed to the supernatural, the divine—a sense it still has.

Today it is probably contrasted most often with the synthetic, the artificial. The use of pesticides that may contaminate ground waters is a source of concern to environmentalists today. At an earlier time, when the population was not so large as it is now, the earth's natural resources would in many cases have had time to replenish themselves. Today, the harvesting of timber in the Amazon rain forests or in the foothills of the Himalayas is a source of perhaps irreversible damage to many species whose usefulness (for medicine, for example) is still unknown, as well as of a loss of soil that supports human and animal populations at the present time.

The words 'rational nature', then, would not have meant the same thing to Boethius as to Aristotle, since Boethius was thinking in a Christian universe of discourse, in which he was using words that would apply to divine and angelic as well as human beings. His use of 'nature' is thus clearly extended beyond the strictly Aristotelian sense—complicated as this is itself. Nonetheless, if only because 'nature' in this strict sense can be applied to bodily beings as such, it is worthwhile considering this sense here.

Since neither nature as an internal source of motion and rest, nor intellectual powers are accessible to the senses, each must be argued to, and the argument must begin with a consideration of the meaning of the terms being used. The intellectual powers being discussed here would be classed by Aristotle as qualities of the person. Hence a general discussion of quality will follow that of nature.

THE NATURE OF NATURE

Aristotle is eminently a naturalist. The notion of nature is quite central to his physical and metaphysical worlds, and to the extent that his is a "natural law" ethics, to the worlds of ethics and politics as well.[1]

Aristotle's word for nature, *physis*, derives from the Greek word, *phuein*, meaning "to spring up." Aristotle arrives at his definition of nature by distinguishing, among things in the world, those that exist by nature from those that exist through other causes, such as art, *techne*. What distinguishes those that exist by nature from the others is that each of the natural beings has in itself its own proper principle of motion and rest. Thus Aristotle defines nature as a "principle and cause of being moved and of rest in the thing to which it belongs primarily and in virtue of that thing, but not accidentally."[2] (This definition is given in terms of "efficient cause.") To have a nature is to have such a principle.[3] Aristotle says further that each thing having such a principle is a substance.[4] Thus for Aristotle, nature means primarily the essence or core or substance of the existing thing—what serves as source of its "motion and rest."

Not everything in the world is equally equipped to move or cease to move, even though nothing natural lacks motion entirely. Creatures tend to behave in characteristic ways befitting their organizational capacities. Birds fly, snakes crawl, each in accordance with its natural tendency, the thrust given it by its natural equipment, of wings, for example, or lack of them, at birth (*natus*: born). It is not possible to alter a thing's nature, although by means of art it can be refined and cultivated. It is natural for a dog to bark, perhaps impossible for a cat to do so, given the vocal organs of each. A Seeing Eye dog can be trained to be very sensitive and responsive to cues in its environment.

DIFFICULTY OF DETERMINING NATURE:
NEED FOR RESEARCH

What is clearly difficult in such a universe is to find out just what is natural to each kind of being, and what may be the result of other factors, such as environment. Aristotle himself devoted considerable attention to such questions, reputedly collecting specimens of various kinds of animals and writing such works as *On Parts of Animals* and *On Motion of Animals*. Today much remains to be learned, not only about the other animals but about the human animal. The current debate about the "naturalness" or not of homosexual behavior illustrates the need to find the physical mechanisms, if they exist, underlying various behaviors.

SUBSTANCE AND NATURE: AGENT AND ACT

From the point of view of nature as a source of action in an actually existing being, one must distinguish the agent, a substantial being, from the act, an accidental feature of that being. Thus a human being can be recognized as one existing thing through time, and yet the source of many different, distinct, and, at times, perhaps contrary actions. In this sense 'substance' and 'nature' may in a given instance indicate one reality, though this reality is seen from two different viewpoints in the case of the use of the two words.

The person, or substantial agent, acts according to his or her nature, although perhaps a nature refined by artistic cultivation. Moreover, the action perfects the agent, so that even though a given act may be, from the metaphysical point of view, dependent upon the substantial agent who performs it, still that act, say the heroic loss of life in rescuing another person, may ultimately bring the person or agent to a completeness that she would otherwise lack.[5]

NATURE: FORMAL, FINAL, MATERIAL CAUSE

Having defined nature in terms of efficient causality, as a principle of motion, Aristotle proceeds in his *Physics* to discuss the various meanings of 'nature' as it is commonly used. These include the essential constituent parts of the being: for example, not only the bear, but the matter or body of the bear, with claws and teeth that enable it to behave in a bearish manner (an explanation in terms of "material" cause). Not only such physical attributes, however, but the frame of mind that accompanies them can be called the "nature" ("formal" cause) of the beast. Is a wolf inherently or naturally a fierce, predatory animal, or is it naturally adapted to be befriended by human beings? This is the sort of question that can only be answered by empirical research.

In a sense the goal or end of a plant or animal (Aristotle's "final cause") can be seen as its nature, indeed as defining it: Do bees exist to make honey? Is the purpose of the bee to serve the ends of human beings? To those who see persons as what is "most perfect in all nature,"[6] it may not seem extravagant to make that claim. For Aristotle, the universe as a whole serves as a goal for the things in it, individuals existing for the sake of the species and species existing to perfect the universe.

These and other similar meanings of 'nature' are for Aristotle the basis of his discussion of things that "spring up" in the world. That discussion culminates in the arguments for an Unmoved Mover at the end of the *Physics*, and prepares for the treatment of such a being, as well as of being itself, in the *Metaphysics*, and also of the soul, in *De Anima*. The method of the latter work is worth looking at in some detail.

NATURE AND THE SOUL

In *De Anima*, Aristotle seeks a definition of the soul, the existence of which he knows from the fact that living things, having a source of motion within themselves, differ from inanimate creatures like stones that need to be moved by something distinct from themselves.

After considering the questions that need to be raised about the soul, he considers the views of his predecessors, people like Democritus, who said that "soul is a sort of fire and hot," and the Pythagoreans who identify soul with the motes in the air or something similar. Anaxagoras says the soul moves things, Plato that the soul is made of the elements and of number.[7]

That these accounts are insufficient is shown, among other things, by the fact that they seem to make any body suitable for any soul, whereas in fact "each art should use its own instruments, and each soul should use its own body."[8]

Aristotle also wishes to consider the various "powers" of different kinds of souls: of plants, to grow, of animals to move about, and so on. His method of pursuing these questions is for the most part inductive. He begins by noting that certain kinds of objects—colors, for example—require a power of a certain sort to grasp them: the eyes to see the color, ears to hear the sound. From the activity, he infers the power to perform it. Similarly, the activities of remembering and imagining evidently require powers of memory and imagination, even though these are not so obviously visible as are the external senses.

A similar method is used in his search for a definition of the soul itself. In this effort, Aristotle gives two different definitions of soul. Seen in terms of its functions, the soul is the seat or source of the vital activities we can observe: that by which primarily we live, and sense, and move, and think.[9] Another way to look at it is to see the soul as the "first actuality of a physically organized body potentially alive,"[10] that is, what makes the body as a whole a living being. The notions of act and potentiality, the ability to do or be and the capacity for that ability, are used here as in the examination of the powers and their activities. The emphasis in this latter definition however is upon the fundamental actuating of the living thing by its soul, fitted to vivify the various organs with which the body is furnished. Looked at abstractly, these organs need an impulse to give them the vital functions they are fitted to perform.

One might ask the question, Does not the brain make the heart beat, and the lungs supply the brain with oxygen, and the heart keep the lungs supplied with blood? Why is some outside impulse needed to get the process started? From the very statement of the question, however, it becomes clear that the various organs do indeed influence one another, but that it is only a living organ that can do this. Each organ, considered as not yet alive, is unable to give the vital push to the others needed for them to function. To look to any one of these powers as giving an ultimate explanation for the existence of life is to enter a circle that results in no logical justification. The question is frequently asked in the form: When is someone dead? Is the lack of breathing or the lack of brain function as detected on machines sufficient to indicate death?

To explain the fact that the various organs in a living thing interact in an orderly, organized way, without any one of them serving as the ultimate reason for this interaction, Aristotle finds it necessary to posit the existence of a soul, a principle distinct from the body of the living thing, not material as is the body, and so not directly dependent upon the organs for its functioning. The souls of the beast and the plant, however, are so immersed in matter that when the functioning of the organs is no longer feasible, these souls simply cease to exist. What is to be said of the soul of the human being?

THE HUMAN SOUL

In a rather mysterious statement in his work *On the Generation of Animals*,[11] Aristotle seems to indicate that the intelligent human soul may enter the body "from without" and thus be in a different situation from the other souls that are simply drawn from the potentiality of the matter of which the animal or plant is composed. The precise meaning and import of this Aristotelian statement has been much discussed; but if it is taken to mean that the human soul is spiritual, that is, not made out of matter and not directly dependent upon matter for its existence, this would accord well with the idea that thinking, as presented above, is able to deal with notions, like that of substance, that lack any precise material correlate.

The soul, then, in Aristotle's view, is itself substantial, and in human beings, it makes with the matter of the body one substance, *this* human being. It functions, however, not directly, (or else it would be doing all it can do all the time: singing, whistling, skipping, thinking: since it is always in act or actually existing and functioning), but through the powers that enable it to do what the being can do. Thus the powers permit intermittent activity, whereas the soul by definition is what keeps the being constantly alive.

What follows from this is that the powers cannot be identical with the soul. They must be distinct from it, and related as potentialities to the various actions that the person can perform. The powers, and the acts performed through them, are "accidents"; the soul is the "substance."[12]

NATURE AND ESSENCE; SUBSTANCE AND ACCIDENTS

Natures belong concretely to individuals, as the source of these individuals' typical activities. But since all members of a species have a common nature by definition, "nature" can be said to be a universal notion. Species differ precisely in their typical abilities to do certain things, and so dogs differ from cats in their abilities, being unable to climb trees, for example.

Dogs can be said to be of a different nature from cats because of the distinctive abilities of the two sorts of animals. Looked at from another point of view, these abilities reveal what each kind of being is: its essence or what the definition answers to. The nature properly expresses the source of a thing's characteristic *activity*; the essence is what the *definition* describes.

Quite distinct from the nature or essence or substance of anything are its "accidents." These are, as Roderick Chisholm has said of sense-data, "what we might call 'ontological parasites'. They are not entities in their own right; they are 'parasitical upon' other things. And what they are parasitical *upon* are persons or selves."[13]

THE ACCIDENT OF QUALITY

Quality, for Aristotle, is the accident that makes a being "such and such," and is what is most able to reveal the nature or essence of a thing. Red objects produce rays falling on the red part of the spectrum; a being possessing the quality of intellect (because of belonging to the sort of being that is capable of understanding—i.e., an intellectual nature or soul) will be able, in optimum circumstances, to produce acts of intellectual insight. Less than optimum circumstances include, for example, being comatose.

HABITS AS QUALITIES

Qualities are what make something be of a certain sort. But, Aristotle points out, there are many kinds of qualities, and he distinguishes four.[14] The first mentioned, habit, is a permanent or stable disposition, (to be distinguished from the second kind of quality, a disposition of a nonpermanent character). This first kind of quality includes in particular intellectual habits. A student of a specific science can be said to be disposed to know biology, for example; but the expert in biology has more than this passing disposition of the student: she habitually understands her science and its details. Habit and disposition are qualities that make an individual human being such as she or he is. The doctrine of habit is of fundamental importance in the understanding of Aristotle's treatment of the sciences and in the elaboration of his ethics, in which he defines virtue as a "state of character," or habit, and in which he discusses in detail the classes of intellectual and moral habits or virtues.

Habits are acquired by practice. The same individual at first is not a scientist and then later, as a result of study and research, is one. Similarly one becomes wise and an artist and even a prudent person through practice.

One intellectual habit or virtue that requires no practice is the habit of understanding, what could be called good sense, the immediate apprehension of the fact that, for example, two things equal to a third thing are equal to each other. This sort of understanding is presupposed to the development of any scientific knowledge such as mathematics.

That Aristotle sees human beings as essentially social and political animals is fundamental to his doctrines of ethics and politics. This is the sphere of action and of the moral virtues, and here the habit or virtue of prudence is central. The prudent person becomes such not simply by theoretical considerations like those of the mathematician but especially by acting prudently upon many occasions. A prudent person knows what action is to be performed in each situation and is able to perform it readily because of long habituation. Aristotle analyzes the various kinds of actions possible to human beings and sums them up under general headings: justice, a good habit which deals with relations between human beings and is required for social and political life; courage (especially of a soldier in battle); and moderation, a good habit dear to all the Greeks, to judge from their literature.

DISPOSITIONS

By dispositions, Aristotle means "qualities . . . easily displaced, or [which] change quickly."[15] Health, for example, unlike the habit of knowing geometry, is a disposition that can be readily changed when one becomes ill, "unless [it] happens to become after a long time so deep-rooted as to be incurable or very difficult to displace, in which case perhaps it should then be called a 'habit'."[16] A human being, Aristotle continues, can be called "naturally healthy" who has an innate disposition to health that is difficult to alter.

Other qualities are more palpable, like hot or wet or red. In each case, a quality identifies an individual. This individual is said to be a "substance," qualified in a variety of ways.

Some people would take the retarded and fetuses to be less than persons because they perform less well. Even though some comatose people do nothing to prove their intellectual ability, however, it happens from time to time that some of them come out of it and perform well again—showing that the accident of intellectual power was there all along, awaiting the right circumstances; and of course the substance capable of supporting it was there, too.

What is perhaps by now evident from the above considerations is that for Aristotle, unlike Confucius, nature was a subject of intense interest, and the sciences he helped develop were a means to understand the various natural functions. It is in this setting of a natural world knowable to human beings that the notion of the human person was able to flourish, centuries after Aristotle, in a way that, for some reason, it did not in the East.[17]

That qualities have a bearing upon human personality and grow out of the nature each person has, seems evident. In particular, the qualities that enable human beings to experience emotions and engage in thinking are revelatory of the essential nature of human personality, as Max Scheler saw in his philosophy of values.[18]

CONCLUSION

The meaning of 'nature' for Aristotle has been explored, as well as the use of qualities of things as means of revealing their natures. The substantial being, "this man, this horse," can be defined thanks to a knowledge of each one's distinctive action or quality. When a person can distinguish red from green, one can infer that the person is not color-blind with reference to these colors, that is, that the person has the normal ability to see in this regard. The act of seeing here described, and the inferred ability, are both "accidents" of the person seen as substance, and they reveal the nature of the substantial being or person as that of a normal human being.

Through such analyses of human behavior, one can come to see the human being as in part explicable in terms of Aristotle's various avenues of explanation, the "four causes," that is, the matter of which things are composed, the efficient cause or source of motion and rest, the form that gives them their distinctive accidental and essential shape, and the final cause or purpose of each. (An example of the last would be the search for the influence of each gene upon human development.) Omitted here is the agent cause considered as external source of the thing's being.

The remaining chapters in Part 3 will illustrate ways in which the other categories of accident cast some light upon the meaning of human personality.

NOTES

1. See Jonathan Barnes, *Aristotle* (New York: Oxford University Press, 1982). John McKenzie, *A Theology of the Old Testament* (Garden City, NY: Doubleday & Company, 1974), 195–96, says that "There is no idea of nature and no word for nature either in Akkadian or in the Old Testament." Taoism lacked a logic with which to study nature systematically. See Donald J. Munro, *The Concept of Man in Early China* (Stanford, CA: Stanford University Press, 1969), 117: "Taoist writings, like those of Confucius and others, have no systematic argument from premise to conclusion. . . ." The development of the meaning of the term 'nature' is one of the principal themes of Aristotle's *Physics* (for example, 2.1–2, where it is contrasted with art and also with the realms of metaphysics and mathematics, respectively). On Thomas Aquinas's use of 'nature', see James A. Weisheipl, *The Development of*

Physical Theory in the Middle Ages (New York: Sheed & Ward, 1959) and his article in Lawrence D. Roberts, ed., *Approaches to Nature in the Middle Ages* (Binghamton, NY: Center for Medieval and Early Renaissance Studies, 1982), 149.

2. Aristotle *Physics* in *Aristotle Selected Works*, trans. Hippocrates G. Apostle and Lloyd P. Gerson (Grinnell, IA: The Peripatetic Press, 1982), 2.1.192b22–24.

3. Aristotle *Physics* 2.1.192b32–34.

4. Ibid., 192b34–35.

5. Karol Wojtyla has discussed the "Person-act," emphasizing the fact that the person in a sense is self-creating by reason of action. See George Huntston Williams, *The Mind of John Paul II* (New York: The Seabury Press, 1981), Chaps. 5 and 8, and 146–54, 190–92, 207, et passim, and Andrew N. Woznicki, *A Christian Humanism: Karol Wojtyla's Existential Personalism* (New Britain, CT: Mariel Publications, 1980), 13–17, 27, 43, 47, and 51.

6. Thomas Aquinas, *Summa Theologiae*, I, Qu. 29, 3, c.

7. *Aristotle's On the Soul*, trans. with Commentaries and Glossary by Hippocrates G. Apostle (Grinnell, IA: The Peripatetic Press, 1981) 1.1–3.

8. Ibid., 407b25–27.

9. Aristotle *On the Soul* 2.1–2.412b4–25; 414a4–14. This is a definition in terms of Aristotle's formal cause, arrived at inductively.

10. Ibid., 2.1.412a25–30.

11. Aristotle *On the Generation of Animals* 3.736b27.

12. By the very fact of my being an individual substance having a rational nature, my nature itself is individuated. Thus while it may be true that human beings in general require food and that wheat is food for human beings, it can be the case that for me as an individual, wheat is indigestible and so not really food for me. Questions about "natural law" as it applies to individuals need to be considered in this light.

13. Chisholm, *Person and Object*, 51.

14. Aristotle *Categories* 8.8b25–11a39. Aristotle distinguishes four classes of qualities: habits, dispositions, affections, and figure or shape. The first two are of particular interest here.

15. Ibid., 8.8b35–36.

16. Ibid., 8.9a2–4.

17. For a discussion of the need to ground the notion of person in that of nature, in a world of known lawfulness, see C. McCall, *Concepts of Person*, Chaps. 13 and 14.

18. See John H. Nota, *Max Scheler: The Man and His Work*, 40: "Scheler's title, . . . *Formalism in Ethics and the Material Ethics of Value* . . . indicates that in opposition to the formal attitude in Kant's ethics, he proposes to offer an ethics directed toward contents and values. The subtitle . . . underscores Scheler's positive intent: 'A New Attempt at Founding an Ethical Personalism.'"

9

Quantity, Place, and Position
as Personal Categories

To have a body is to have a present.
—Maurice Merleau-Ponty

Quantity is like "place" and "position"—or situation of limbs in relation to the whole body—a category that can be applied to many other bodily beings besides persons. But each of them also sheds light on the nature of human personhood. These categories will now be considered in turn.

QUANTITY

'Quantity' is the word Aristotle uses to denote predicates that refer to a body's having "parts outside parts," that is, being spread out in space, unlike, say, a spiritual being or a mathematical point.[1] As the body, particularly the face, is the means of a person's being present in the world and communicating with others (consider the expression, "in my face" as meaning too aggressively present to me), it is fundamentally important to human beings and human society.[2]

Boethius, in defining person as an "individual substance of a rational nature," was apparently trying to provide a kind of generic definition of 'person', one that would apply to purely spiritual persons such as angels or the divine Persons, as well as to human beings. Something of the same wish to be inclusive may also govern Locke's definition of person, which makes no mention of bodily parts: "a thinking intelligent being, that has reason and reflection, and can consider itself as itself, the same thinking thing, in different times and places."[3]

But the Lockean definition also reflects the sort of split in the human being that has affected many discussions of the person in recent centuries, following Descartes's *Meditations*, 6, with its consideration of the human being as essentially a "thinking thing," with the bodily "extended thing" inexplicably joined to it.

98

The overly "spiritual" Lockean definition tends to deprive the person of the spontaneity and givenness inherent in everything connected with matter, which is at once dependable and unpredictable. The very firmness of rock can give way without warning in an earthquake. David Wiggins speaks well of the "excessively constructional approach to the subject of person (constructional, . . . in contrast with descriptive). . . ."[4] Things composed of matter, including human beings, are measurable by quantity; and bodily beings have a certain element of surprise built into them.

Is it essential to the notion of a microbe that it be small? Could there be an elephant-sized microbe? It seems that this would, properly speaking, amount to a contradiction in terms. While the quantity itself may seem somewhat trivial in relation to human personality, it is in fact fraught with significance for the individual human being—and for the earth on which human beings exist. Thomas Aquinas identifies the "designated quantity of primary matter" as a principle of individuation in material things, that is, what enables one of two identical twins, for example, to be individually distinct from the other.

When the empirical quantity of the human body is considered in relation to that of other human beings or of the earth, questions of conservation and justice arise. If North Americans consume 40 percent of the world's products it is unlikely that the rest of the world's population will ever rise to the standard of living of the United States. More likely is a reduction in U.S. patterns of consumption in the century ahead.

PERSONS: MATTER AND SPIRIT

If the human person (considered apart from any purely spiritual divine or angelic persons) is necessarily animal, then to define one as purely spiritual is to contradict oneself in the very act of defining. But if the person is animal, how does this affect the question of "personal immortality"?

For Thomas Aquinas, the question has a straightforward answer: the human soul, after its separation from the body, retains a kind of inclination for this individual body sufficient for it to remain individualized as this person, even though, strictly speaking, it is itself not a person but only part of a person.[5]

If, on the other hand, one defines the person as simply the intelligent part of a human being, then one has the problem of explaining the Cartesian union of this mind or soul with the body, and the attendant problems of explaining how one person perdures through many bodily changes and how body and soul interact.

Nothing, perhaps, tells more about the relationship, sometimes uneasy, between body and soul, than does the problem of addiction: human beings can become enslaved to various naturally occurring objects in the world or can create for themselves artificial objects which they then make the focus of all their efforts. Freedom from such enslavement no doubt requires constant vigilance, although this freedom ideally should not be purchased at the price of all spontaneous venturing into the world.

Even apart from the speculations of modern philosophers on the nature of the bond and the interaction between mind and body, there remains the hope of attaining a deeper understanding of human beings through documenting the modes of interaction between soul or mind and body. Especially in the field of psychosomatic medicine, new information is constantly becoming available on the precise physiological pathways of influence between mind and body.[6] The therapeutic use of biofeedback in healing processes has developed from scientific understanding of just these relationships. A challenge to all future researchers in this field will be to explain how a thought, or even just an inclination, comes to be translated into bodily symptoms.

PLACE

In speaking of place (or "where") as a category, Aristotle has in mind the relation of a body to its container, of water, for example, to the glass that contains it, specifically to the inside of the glass. Place is defined as the inner surface of the surrounding body. Whatever I take to be the surrounding body—the inside of a house, for example, or the walls of the room in which I am sitting—provides a location or place in which I am to be found. While it may be thinkable that there be but one body (if the universe be thought of as one being, including all its galaxies), nevertheless, in the universe as we encounter it, bodies have places in which they are contained. There would appear to be no way to be a human being and not occupy a place.

The philosopher Christopher Gill notes that "Both themes ["living creatures have a natural inclination to pursue their own good, . . . and care for others of their kind"] form part of the Stoic doctrine of *oikeiosis* (an untranslatable term which implies both assimilating oneself to the world and making the world one's own); . . ."[7] One of the very first things that occurs in the life of the new conceptus is movement to its proper place, and this implantation in the womb—*oikeiosis*—provides the sole expectation of its normal development. From that point on, a suitable place is important to each human being's welfare.[8] Astronauts depend for survival upon the integrity of the space craft—the place in which they fly.

It has been noted that Gabriel Marcel gives considerable attention to the notion of "situation." Martin Heidegger refers to his human existent being as "Dasein," literally "being there."[9] Gaston Bachelard has explored the meaning of such words as 'nook', 'attic', 'cellar', and their connotations for the life experience of human beings.[10]

From whatever angle the notion is considered, the fact is that place exerts a profound influence upon a person.[11] A person may devote an entire lifetime to finding the proper place. While there are individual differences in the amount of dependence human beings have upon the places they occupy, for most people it is wrenching to be uprooted and sent into exile by war or some other social or physical catastrophe. On the other hand, freedom to move at will to a more favorable place is also important.

Freedom of assembly in a common place is important for the exercise of democratic political responsibilities and rights, and abridging this freedom is often one of the first acts of a tyrannical regime. There are both ethical and spiritual implications to the notion of place: the person who falsely shouts "fire!" in a crowded place endangers the safety of everyone there; the condition of persons who for reasons of asceticism decide to remain homeless, like the Jain monks and nuns of India, makes clear the imposed and inescapable hardship of people who, because of their condition of homelessness, lack the shelter and the rootedness a permanent place can provide.

Architecture can be understood as providing a means to the pursuit of a particular kind of life. Certain architectural barriers prevent the maximum participation of human beings in the social life of their group. Much recent discussion has centered upon the withering effect upon neighborhoods of badly located freeways, for example. The castle was constructed in medieval times precisely to make unwelcomed entrances difficult. Kafka's *Castle* uses the building as a symbol of the impossibility of access by one who is not recognized in a society.

Finally, there are places, like times, seen as sacred because they are sites and occasions of divine encounter. Most often these are places of impressive natural beauty or grandeur such as mountain tops and rivers. Temples and monuments are often erected in such places to commemorate the divine encounter.[12]

POSITION

The various bodily positions a human being can assume tell much about that person's approach to life. A child in the womb must change positions constantly in order to develop normally. This flow of movement continues in the newborn, where the encounter with things in the world seems to take place through the apparently random kicks and flailings that fill the baby's waking hours.

Upright posture is generally considered to have evolutionary significance. A two-year-old in the lotus position in Asia can rock back and forth, asleep, like a top, without actually falling. The yogi with years of practice in adopting the same posture can maintain a contact with the earth and with the social scene around him for many hours at a time with little fatigue. Kneeling and bowing speak of reverence and respect for the person being encountered, as does the Indian gesture of the "anjali," in which hands are joined with palms pressed together before the face.[13]

Integral to the idea of position, of course, is that of the relation of limbs to the body as a whole; but the whole body is held in place by the force of gravity, a pull upon my body by another body, notably the earth. Such a concept of gravity was unknown to Aristotle. For Aristotle, the center of the universe is the center of the earth.

Astronauts need to learn to live in a weightless situation in which it is hard to distinguish up from down. A baby tossed into the air by its parent seems to enjoy the momentary feeling of weightlessness. Acrobats push to the limit the ability of the body to "defy gravity."

CONCLUSION

As will be evident from a consideration of quantity, place, and position, these categories name important forces in the life of the human person. Even though they seem less central to the notion of human personality than other categories (like substance and relation), they nonetheless have their own contribution to make to the understanding of human personhood.

NOTES

1. Aristotle, *Categories*, trans. H. G. Apostle, 6.4b20: "Of quantities, some are discrete but others are continuous. . . . Examples of a discrete quantity are a [whole] number and speech; examples of a continuous quantity are a line, a surface, a body, and, besides these, time and place."

2. See Maurice Merleau-Ponty, *Phenomenology of Perception*, trans. Colin Smith (Atlantic Highlands, NJ: Humanities Press, 1962), 78, note 2; see also S. B. Rosenthal and Patrick L. Bourgeois, *Mead and Merleau-Ponty* (Albany, NY: State University of New York Press, 1994).

3. John Locke, *An Essay Concerning Human Understanding*, II, xxvii, 2. Risieri Frondizi points out, in *The Nature of the Self: A Functional Interpretation* (New Haven: Yale University Press, 1953), 44–45: "that of the two senses in which the concept of substance could be taken—*res per se subsistens* and *substans accidentibus*—Locke chose the second, thus greatly facilitating the process of the disintegration of substance." And, 26: "in the *Essay* he is not concerned with substance but with the *idea* of substance . . .;" and finally, 32: "for one who has a substantialist concept . . . [p]ersonal identity is based securely upon substantial identity. Locke does not, however, choose this way out."

4. David Wiggins, "Personal Identity," in his *Sameness and Substance*, (Oxford: Basil Blackwell, 1980), 163.

5. For a less strictly metaphysical approach to the notion of human personhood than is to be found in the *Summa of Theology*, see Thomas Aquinas, *The Literal Exposition on Job: A Scriptural Commentary Concerning Providence*, trans. Anthony Damico, The American Academy of Religion Classics in Religious Studies (Atlanta, GA: Scholars Press, 1989), for example, on 3, 11–17, p. 107.

6. See, for example, Sandra Blakeslee, "Complex and Hidden Brain in the Gut Makes Stomachaches and Butterflies," *The New York Times*, January 23, 1996, Sec. C, 1–3: "the body has two brains—the familiar one encased in the skull and the lesser

known but vitally important one found in the human gut." (1) The latter is "a network of neurons, neurotransmitters and proteins ... support cells like those found in the brain proper and a complex circuitry that enables it to act independently, learn, remember and, as the saying goes, produce gut feelings." (1) "[t]he two nervous systems [are] connected via the vagus nerve" (3).

7. Christopher Gill, "The Human Being as an Ethical Norm," *The Person and the Human Mind: Issues in Ancient and Modern Philosophy* (Oxford: Clarendon Press, 1990), 133.

8. The tragic phenomenon of "crib deaths" of infants calls attention to the need for a fitting place (and position) for a very young human being.

9. See Martin Heidegger, *Being and Time*, trans. John Macquarrie and Edward Robinson (New York: Harper & Row, 1962).

10. Gaston Bachelard, *The Poetics of Space*, trans. Maria Jolas (Boston: Beacon Press, 1969).

11. Jeff Malpas, "A Taste of Madeleine: Notes Towards a Philosophy of Place," *International Philosophical Quarterly* 34, 4 (December 1994): 433–51, discusses the question of the meaning of place for human beings.

12. Max Scheler considered the relation to the divine to be the most important defining relationship of human persons. See John H. Nota, *Max Scheler: The Man and His Works* (Chicago: Franciscan Herald Press, 1983), 92–93, et passim.

13. According to Max Scheler in his last period, the God of one who kneels is different from the God of one who sits or stands. See Nota, *Scheler*, 131.

10

Persons in Relationships

It turns out, then, that relationality and substantiality go together as two
distinct but inseparable modes of reality.

—W. Norris Clarke

PERSONS IN SOCIETY: RELATION A PECULIAR CATEGORY

Because human beings are social by nature, needing to grow up in the presence
of other human beings to function normally as adults, the question arises: is it
in virtue of social relationships that human beings can be called persons?[1]

A difficulty immediately presents itself to one who considers this possibility:
it seems that for a relationship to exist, two or more objects must be present to
be related.[2] Mother and child are existing beings and, at the same time, from
a different but equally necessary point of view, related. A "chicken and egg"
puzzle presents itself here. There is no way the child can come to exist apart
from its mother's and father's action; yet this new being is identical only with
itself, not with its progenitors. The child is a substantial being in its own right,
with a distinct set of genes, for example, different from those of either parent.
The child is related to its parents as their offspring; the parents are related to
the child as the source of its being. Yet each of the three persons involved here
is a distinct individual in its own right.

For Aristotle, relationship was a category different from the other accidental
categories in that relation is not only *in* the substance, but it also involves
reference *to* another. Annie's relation of being smaller than Liz not only implies
something in Annie, as do all accidents, but it is necessarily something that is
referred *to* Liz, from which circumstance it gets its Greek name, "toward something."[3] A peculiarity of the accident of relation is the fact that in a sense
many of the categories, like position, can be said to be instances of relation.[4]

In the consideration of medieval writers on the person (Chapter 5), it has
been pointed out that it was Richard of Saint Victor who particularly emphasized the importance of relation in reference to personhood. It must surely be
said that no human person could exist entirely unrelated: each human being

104

has parents. For many contemporary thinkers, however, it seems that if persons are related, they cannot properly be called substances.[5] This question involves epistemological issues that need not be considered here: knowledge itself involves a relation between the knower and the thing known.

SUBSTANCE AND RELATION: PHENOMENOLOGY AND STRUCTURALISM

Perhaps one reason Aristotle's "substance" has fallen into disfavor, compared to accidents, is the current use of the phenomenological method, invented by Edmund Husserl, but never completely worked out by him. This method aims to get beyond fascination with elaborate metaphysical theories by putting them into brackets, "on hold" as it were, and concentrating instead upon the "thing itself," which presents itself to the attentive consciousness. In his meticulous examination of phenomena, the phenomenologist looks only at what actually appears with overwhelming evidence, refusing to be committed as to the ultimate metaphysical or even physical structure that may account for this appearance. Gabriel Marcel, a practitioner of this method, while professing puzzlement at the notion of substance, is inclined to see it as getting in the way of an understanding of personhood, which for him is eminently relational.

Phenomenology seen as a method rather than as an alternate metaphysics, however, would seem not to impugn the notion of substance but rather to sidestep the entire question. Something similar can be said about structuralism as interpreted by, for example, Jean Piaget. Structuralists search out the various levels at which structures can be discerned in given realities, without attempting to find any sort of "ultimate agent."[6]

For a complete theory of human personality today, however, account must be taken of the contributions of phenomenology. Max Scheler, Edith Stein, and Karol Wojtyla are among the thinkers who have offered theories of the nature of person in a phenomenological setting.

Karol Wojtyla sees the person as self-constituting through action, but at the same time he criticizes Scheler for failing to work out a sufficient metaphysical basis for personality.[7] Both Scheler and Wojtyla, however, are interested in the person as a moral agent, and, therefore, in the mature human person. Scheler observes that

> [e]ven if . . . we broaden the concept of the person and grant that there are seeds of personhood in still-undeveloped levels of human beingness (e.g., in children or imbeciles), there remains the fact that the place . . . in which the nature of the person first flashes before us is to be sought only in a certain *kind* of man, not man in general. . . .[8]

Like Max Scheler, who founded his ethics of value upon an appreciation of feelings, rather than simply upon the rationality of the Kantian "formal" ethics,

Edith Stein sought to come to an understanding of the human person through feelings like that of joy.[9]

RELATIONS: PSYCHOLOGICAL, GENDERED, AND PHYSICAL

It is in the matter of human psychological development, perhaps, that the notion of relationship is seen as most important today. The way in which a person is brought up by their parents can have a lifelong influence upon that individual's way of coping with the challenges of life.[10]

The philosopher Prudence Allen has explored the notion of analogy as a way of understanding how, at the most fundamental level, human beings can be considered as systems of relationships and related to one another, and in particular, how men are related to women. It is neither the case that women are completely like men nor that they are altogether different: the situation is rather that there is a noteworthy difference along with a fundamental likeness.[11]

The fact that the human body is so constructed that a person has a certain perspective upon the world seems to imply the necessity for human beings to interact constructively with one another: what one lacks, for example in sight, can to some extent be supplied by others.[12]

No doubt there are natural factors, many of them perhaps still unknown, that influence the development of the human person. Research in evolutionary biology indicates that numerous human personality traits may be rooted in anatomical and physiological factors common to many animal species. A Japanese thinker has theorized that there is a correlation between climate and human personality.[13] The signs of the zodiac may reflect the perception of such a relationship at a prescientific level. Environmental and ecological issues inevitably impinge upon the lives of human persons, as is noted in Chapter 8.

SOCIAL, POLITICAL, AND ECONOMIC RELATIONS

Human beings need social and political association for their very existence, according to Aristotle. The man without a hearth or a tribe is somehow an outcast, unable to reach the full perfection of virtuous living for which he is destined.[14] Relations with a political society, for Aristotle fundamental in human nature, since "man is by nature a political animal," can be seen as the basis for the "legal person," the human being seen as a legal entity. It is the basis for recognition by the state of the corporation as an agent in legal transactions. Were one to deny any substantial character to the individual human being, the society, notably the state, would seem to be the obvious candidate to absorb the substantial characteristics denied the individual. In a totalitarian state, human beings are treated as if they were mere parts of the greater reality of the whole society. Thus, China today sees the Dalai Lama's recognition of a small boy as the reincarnation of an earlier Buddhist leader as an act of defiance against the Chinese state.[15]

The question of human rights is primarily a matter of relationships. Aristotle did not devote the attention to questions of the protection of human rights that later thinkers did, particularly those who evolved the theory of English Common Law. For many of these thinkers, the most effective protection for the individual citizen against the usurpation of rights by the state is to be found in the strengthening of lesser societies, notably the family, the church, and other voluntary organizations. The law itself, especially the constitution of a state, can in practice be the most powerful protection of the citizen and his rights, as Thomas More points out in Robert Bolt's drama, "A Man for All Seasons."

The early Marx and some Eastern European marxists (e.g., Karel Kosik and Mihailo Markovic) have devoted considerable attention to the question of the preservation of human rights in a society that is totally organized for production and distribution.[16]

Marx saw human labor as creating not only capital, but the worker himself. In a celebrated passage in Hegel's *Phenomenology of Mind* the slave is seen to liberate himself and eventually his master through his own work, thus making himself a creator.

Probably the most effective critique of a totally organized society is to be found, however, in the arts, in play, and in leisure, which Josef Pieper saw as the basis of religious practice and of all culture.[17]

Undoubtedly the most pressing social problem facing the entire world at the present time is that of establishing economic relationships that will benefit all human beings. The growing use of robots and techniques of production and information retrieval that eliminate human beings from the need to be involved in production and service carries with it the urgent necessity for finding a way to distribute to every human being the means of livelihood that each one needs. What had been a result unseen by most Europeans and Americans, the enslavement of whole populations by the greed of a few persons, is now evident to all through television.

Because a human being can be self-conscious, it is possible in a sense for one to be related to oneself: I to me. As a result, I can be instrumental in raising my own level of consciousness or awareness of my situation in relation to society or to the world. I can thus have a hand in shaping my own life history through becoming more aware of my lacks and needs, as well as my accomplishments.

CONCLUSION

It is clear that the substantially existing human person is also a being related to other things and persons.[18] These relationships are most obvious in the family and among friends, for intimate associations, and in political organizations, for larger groups. Chapter 11 will deal with what is acknowledged to be another key to understanding the person: action.

NOTES

1. On the entire question of persons as social beings, see John Macmurray, *Persons in Relation* (Atlantic Highlands, NJ: Humanities Press International, 1991), for example, 61–62: "The human infant, then, born into, and adapted to, a common life with the mother, is a person from birth." And, 170: "My knowledge of another is a function of my love for him; and in proportion as my knowledge is a function of my fear of him, it is illusory and unreal."

2. Aspects of the things, like "redness," can of course be the immediate subject of the relation: this boy's hair is a deeper shade of red than that one's, for example.

3. Aristotle *Categories* 7.6b7–8. Constantine Cavernos, *The Classical Theory of Relations: A Study in the Metaphysics of Plato, Aristotle and Thomism*, (Belmont, MA: Institute for Byzantine and Modern Greek Studies, 1975) discusses the theory of relations in detail.

4. See Aristotle *Categories* 7.6b2–3.

5. See Peter Smith, "Human Persons," 61–81 in Christopher Gill, ed., *The Person and the Human Mind: Issues in Ancient and Modern Philosophy* (Oxford: Clarendon Press, 1990), 74.

6. Jean Piaget, *Structuralism*, trans. Chaninah Maschler (New York: Basic Books, 1970). On phenomenology as method or metaphysics in relation to the question of the person as speaker, see Patrick A. Bourgeois, "Semiotics and the Deconstruction of Presence: A Ricoeurian Alternative," ACPQ, 66, 3 (summer 1992): 361–97, and "Critical Reflections on 'Object and Phenomenon and the Deconstructed Present'," in ibid. 67, 2 (spring 1993): 253–56, especially 255.

7. See Andrew N. Woznicki, *A Christian Humanism: Karol Wojtyla's Existential Personalism* (New Britain, CT: Mariel Publications, 1980), 9. Wojtyla's "act-person" recalls Scheler's "act-substance."

8. Max Scheler, *Formalism in Ethics and Non-formal Ethics of Value* (Evanston: Northwestern University Press, 1973), 476.

9. See Mary Catherine Basehart, "Edith Stein's Philosophy of Person," in John Sullivan, ed., *Carmelite Studies: Edith Stein Symposium; Teresian Culture* (Washington, DC: ICS Publications, 1987), 39, and, in ibid., John Nota, "Edith Stein and Martin Heidegger," 58: "Now person, according to Edith Stein, is always *Mitsein*—being with. . . ." In her autobiography, Stein says: ". . . I proceeded to a subject of great personal interest which would occupy me in all subsequent writings: the structure of the human person."—cited in Waltraud Herbstrith, *Edith Stein: A Biography*, trans. Bernard Bonowitz (San Francisco: Ignatius Press, 1992), 144 (*Werke*, [Louvain: Nauwaelaerts, 1965], 279). Stein mentions in a letter to Roman Ingarten that she was assisting Husserl in getting his notes ready for publication: *Edith Stein: Self-Portrait in Letters*, trans. Josephine Koeppel (Washington, DC: ICS Publications, 1993), 6: ". . . I have continued working on that draft on my own authority, without running into any opposition about that, and am as far as 'Person.'"—January 28, 1917; (first published in *Philosophy and Phenomenological Research*, 23 [1962]). In the same volume, Letter 21, she writes to Fritz Kaufmann: ". . . I am working at present on the analysis of the person." (23; March 10, 1918). And, in her doctoral dissertation, *On the Problem of Empathy*, trans. Waltraut Stein, (Washington, DC: ICS Publications, 1989), see 106 and following.

10. See Alice Miller, *For Your Own Good: Hidden Cruelty in Childrearing and the Roots of Violence*, trans. Hildegard and Hunter Hannum (New York: Farrar Straus Giroux, 1985). Miller deplores punishment of children as leading to an endless cycle of violence for one generation after another.

11. See Prudence Allan, "A Woman and a Man as Prime Analogical Beings," ACPQ, 66, 4 (Autumn, 1992): 465–82. She is following the thought of the Polish philosopher M. A. Krapiec.

12. See Wilfrid Desan, *The Planetary Man: A Noetic Prelude to a United World* (Washington, DC: Georgetown University Press, 1961), 53–61.

13. Tetsuro Watsuji, *Climate and Culture: A Philosophical Study* (New York: Greenwood Press, 1989).

14. See Aristotle's *Politics* 1.1. John Kirkpatrick and Geoffrey M. White discuss various understandings of 'person' in certain Pacific societies, including a notion of the group as primarily responsible for actions. See "Exploring Ethnopsychologies," in White and Kirkpatrick, *Person, Self, and Experience: Exploring Pacific Ethnopsychologies* (Berkeley: University of California Press, 1985), 11. See also Richard A. Wright, *African Philosophy: An Introduction* (Lanham, MD: University Press of America, 1984), 172: ". . . in the African view it is the community which defines the person, not some isolated static quality of rationality, will, or memory." And, ibid., 163–81 and 205–08; and M. Leenhardt, *Do Kamo: Person and Myth in the Melanesian World*, trans. B. M. Gulati (Chicago: The University of Chicago Press, 1979), xxiii–xxv, and xxxii, note, in addition to 153–69. Marcel Mauss, "A Category of the Human Mind: the notion of person; the notion of self," trans. W. D. Halls, in *The Category of the Person: Anthropology, Philosophy, History*, ed. Michael Carrithers et al. (Cambridge: Cambridge University Press, 1985), discusses the use of 'person' by French anthropologists; first published in *Mélanges de l'Histoire des Religions* (1909).

15. *The New York Times*, May 18, 1995.

16. See Karl Marx, *Grundrisse: Foundations of the Critique of Political Economy*, trans. Martin Nicolano (NY: Random House, 1973), pp. 89, 242–46, et passim; and "On the Jewish Question," *Early Texts*, trans. David McLellan (Oxford: Basil Blackwell, 1971), 107.

17. Josef Pieper, *Leisure, the Basis of Culture*, trans. Alexander Dru (New York: Pantheon Books, 1952).

18. See Robert O. Johann, "The Development of Community," 65–75, in George F. McLean and Hugo Meynell, eds., *Person and Society* (Lanham, MD: University Press of America, 1988), especially 73: "Since life is human only as intentional, . . . the unit of human living is not the solitary ego but 'you and I' in communication. It is a unit that can be properly understood only from the 'inside', . . . And neither the mathematical model of a 'sum' nor the biological model of an 'organism' do it justice. What is required is the distinctly *personal* model of a conversation or a dialogue."

11

Action, Passion, and the Compassionate Buddha

> Actions belong to supposits.
> —Thomas Aquinas

ACTION EAST AND WEST

Mother Teresa of Calcutta and the Vietnam War symbolize, respectively, the contrast between success and failure in the way in which the typical Westerner approaches the challenges of human action and passion. While the intractable problem of homelessness is worldwide, it is a woman with Western values who sees it as her obligation to intervene to try to alleviate the suffering of persons facing death—for Christians, the decisive moment of life, but for the typical person of Oriental culture, one in a perhaps endless series of rounds of death and life. Action—intervening to make things happen—seems to be a natural function of the person of Western heritage.

The bad side of the Western tendency to act is lack of patience in a situation in which action is impossible or meaningless. The quagmire of the Vietnam War, which ended in a U.S. defeat and the abandonment of thousands of U.S. soldiers, with the subsequent effort to reestablish trade relations with Vietnam, relations in which the United States could once again act effectively, illustrates the disadvantage of the West when the matter at stake involves waiting.

On the other hand, Oriental persons accept more easily than do westerners the impossibility of attaining a completely perfect world; they are patient with the way things are, they accept evil as the underside of a life tapestry displaying good on its face. For a Western person, solitary confinement is a dreadful punishment. For a non-Western person, it may be deadly.

The West's increasing fascination with the Orient in modern times can be seen in the philosophy of Arthur Schopenhauer.[1] This pessimistic misogynist assumes that there is no possibility of satisfaction of an endless appetite for

110

pleasure in human beings, so that frustration is the only alternative to a complete detachment from the satisfaction of needs and wants in human beings. In advocating such detachment he echoes the teaching of saintly Eastern figures like the Buddha. Numerous westerners have travelled to the East to sit at the feet of teachers with a reputation for being able to impart the ancient disciplines of meditation.

ACTIONS BELONG TO PERSONS

The human being as agent, worker in the world, doer and maker, is a powerful symbol for the Western mind. The "great man" theory of history holds that a leader like Napoleon can influence the course of world history for centuries. Such a person is not so much made by his time and circumstances as he is the maker of the political world in which he operates.

The predicament of "action" is most generally recognized as revealing the person. The agent or doer is typically understood to be a being who can plan to accomplish an act and who therefore can act intentionally to bring about an end.[2] As a bodily being, the person can bring about a change in the world as the result of a mental plan. One may also operate in a purely mental way, without a visible external outcome, as when one performs mental arithmetic exercises.

Working and patience, action and receptiveness are important indicators of the personhood of the one responsible for them. The mystery of human personality is ultimately involved in the choice each adult makes of a certain kind of life and of the means to be used to achieve it. Whether a person will stand up under torture or betray comrades rather than submit to it; whether or not one will accept discipline for the sake of an important good: each of the myriad decisions of any human being's life at once results from the core of human personhood and helps define the psychological personality we observe in ourselves and others.

Aristotle's complementary categories of action (*poiein*)[3] and passion (*paschein*)[4]— or being acted upon—illustrate salient features of personality, from both its substantial and its relational aspect.

Is an action to be seen as springing from the one who performs it in such a way that it can later be attributed to that individual alone? For Gabriel Marcel, it is a test of a person's authenticity that one stand behind one's actions, able to say, "Yes, it was I who did it." To refuse to do this is to introduce a kind of split into one's being as a person and implicitly to destroy one's integrity. If a person anticipates being forced to do something, Marcel says, he should in advance disavow what may be forced from him.

If Immanuel Kant puts the "transcendental Ego" beyond human comprehension in the *Critique of Practical Reason*, he speaks of a more accessible person in his *Anthropology*.[5]

ACTION AND "MAKING ONE'S MARK"

"Action follows being," says Thomas Aquinas. There is nothing trivial about human action. It is heavy with import from its conception to its completion. Of all human actions, the speech act and the act of reproduction are the most fraught with implication. A word may be said with little reflection but its effect felt for years or decades. J. L. Austin has studied "performative speech acts" like the "I do" spoken in the wedding ceremony.[6]

Despite theories like structuralism that treat language as divorced from the speaker, Paul Ricoeur has argued convincingly for the need to take account, not only of the language system within which a person works, but of the one who is author of the discourse, as well.[7] Sigmund Freud talks about slips of the tongue. Perhaps these indicate a drive in the person toward integrity, toward bringing speech and life into accord. Like the act of speaking, the sexual act as leading to the creation of a new person is similarly a weighty act, even though it may be engaged in without advertence to its nature.

Action theory has recently emphasized the importance of intention in defining human action. The distinction between what Marcel called an "act" and a mere "gesture" is echoed here. Intentional action that involves the body illustrates vividly the wholeness of the human person: Acts belong to the person (or "rational supposit," in the medieval terminology),[8] not to the body alone (or they would not be acts, but mere gestures); but not to the soul alone, either, or they would lack the bodily qualities that make them evident and observable.

In another sense, however, the person considered as a bodily being can influence what happens in the world simply through distinctive bodily deeds. Consider, for example, the possible incompatibility between the blood types of mother and child in the womb. Until a way was found to overcome the results of such lack of compatibility, a fatal outcome to the pregnancy was to be expected. Characteristics like finger- and voice-prints apparently identify a unique human being and in this way can serve to exemplify the contribution that this individual alone can be expected to make in the world. The child in the womb does not plan its blood type, nor do we intend the uniqueness of our finger- or voice-prints. Yet by these means persons might be said to be "making their mark"—establishing their unique presence—in the world.

The principal question regarding action in relation to the person is whether or not a person can be held accountable for actions done. To act in a fully realized human way is to act intentionally: unintended acts or unthinking gestures are not fully "human acts." The law recognizes this in distinguishing between murder as an intended act and manslaughter as the unintentional killing of a human being.

This question of accountability brings up another interesting point of difference between Eastern and Western ways. Eastern persons are often unable to conceive of themselves apart from the group—tribe, class, or caste—into which they are born. They see themselves and are seen by their society as embedded in the social group, whereas a typical person of Western culture finds acting against a group not only thinkable, but entirely possible and at times even necessary. After the assassination of Indira Gandhi in India, mobs took revenge not upon her actual killers, but upon many Sikhs whose only connection with the murderers was that of a common religious belief. Here, as frequently in non-Western societies, it is the group rather than the individual that is held responsible.

The objective morality of an act is primarily determined by the purpose of the act, rather than the purpose of the doer. My purpose in "cornering the market" may be to make money; but if my action defeats the very purpose of the market (to serve as a means of exchange), the act of making money by this means becomes immoral. Severing economics from its moral basis by letting market forces operate without restraint is the source of much of the malaise of capitalism; as Marx pointed out, human beings may then be diminished by the very economic efforts that by definition exist to support human life. In undertaking a work, one undertakes, at the same time, to try to achieve its purpose.

This characteristic of a fully human act bringing about change in the external world illustrates the twofold character of human personality, that of being substantial and relational.

Because "action follows existence,"[9] and the existing thing is a substance, the ultimate doer in any act is, not the trigger finger of the one who fires the gun, nor the power to pull the trigger, but the person who fires. The substantial character of the human agent is thus essential in agency. Thus a series of events needs to take place in the material world for such a thing to happen: brain chemicals need to transmit the results of a perception and the impetus for action along the proper nerve pathways, and the bullet must finally come to rest in a certain place. But the decision to pull the trigger and fire the gun is one that points to a substance of a kind that is spiritual, not simply part of the world in which it functions. The person capable of this sort of action is a spiritual as well as a material substance.

PASSION

'Passion' or 'suffering', for Aristotle, refers to receiving or undergoing the action of an agent: the football receives the action of the punter. Pleasure and pain in this sense are both sufferances.[10] Among the most private of human experiences, they reflect the results of human action as it succeeds or fails. Aristotle, and Plato before him, knew that there are ways of regulating these experiences, the good habits or virtues of moderation and courage, that have important social implications. "Doing drugs" or overindulgence in food or alcohol tend to be private acts, but their public consequences are generally quickly evident, most dramatically in the case of accidents resulting from impaired ability to act prudently. Pleasure seems to indicate that an action is proceeding successfully. The purpose of the action is something distinct from the accompanying pleasure. The attainment of this purpose or end is what the action tends toward "naturally," so that the pleasure is not the end but an accompaniment of efficient action. Psychiatrists and moralists have remarked upon the irony involved in pursuit of pleasure as an end: while undertaking difficult courses of action (like a regimen of exercise) can result in pleasure (through the release of chemical substances in the brain), the attempt to attain unlimited pleasure is doomed to failure; pain always accompanies the pursuit of pleasure.

Mental pain can be the measure of the lack of congruence between the goal I intend and the result I actually accomplish by my action. It thus makes clear the importance of intention in the action. Since pleasure and pain are eminently private experiences, how is it possible for a person to feel with, to sympathize or empathize with another human being? The phenomenologist Edith Stein wrote her doctoral dissertation *On The Problem of Empathy*.[11] In it she argues, against her teachers Husserl and Scheler, that empathy is needed to come to an understanding of another human person, and that the body is necessary for the experience of empathy. Two human beings can be detached observers of the same painting, for example, but when one of them experiences a feeling in reference to it, this at once establishes a kind of texture in the "I" of that person, and makes it possible, as it would not be otherwise, for the other to enter empathetically into that experience of feeling.

The Christian sees in the Passion of Jesus the universal law of suffering for human beings in this life, but always against the background of the realization that this suffering itself has something redemptive about it.[12] Above all, for the Christian, all suffering willingly accepted can have a happy and indeed glorious end, a resurrection to a new and better life, even here and now.

Sympathy is a source of social bonding, but pleasure and pain can be used to separate a person from social and intellectual commitments. Torture and addiction are ways to force human beings to concentrate upon their own experience and its isolating character so as to separate them effectively from a social group. It is because the person is a material substance that one is especially vulnerable to these forces.[13]

Descartes's lifelong struggle with ill health may have favored his theory of a sharp dichotomy between mind and body. And indeed, to a person enduring physical pain and discomfort the body can seem a kind of carapace, interfering with action rather than integrally involved in it. For a person forced by illness to forego the usual use of the limbs, atrophy of muscles can result.[14]

Derek Parfit, like some earlier English thinkers, assumes an excessively Cartesian split between mind and body in posing his questions about human personhood. He says:

I claim that, when we ask what persons are, . . . the fundamental question is
a choice between two views. On one view, we are separately existing entities,
distinct from our brain and bodies. . . .
The other view is the Reductionist View. And I claim that, of these, the
second view is true. . . . *Buddha would have agreed*. . . . the plausible views . . .
agree that we are *not* separately existing entities, distinct from our brains
and bodies, whose existence must be all-or-nothing.
   I claim that a person is not like a Cartesian Ego. . . . A person is like a
nation.[15]

Apart from the matter of whether the Buddha ever considered, in a philosophical way, the question of the nature of the human person, one might note
that it was precisely the experience of pain, even in a bodily sense, that prompted
him to seek a way out of this problem. Spiritual disciplines designed to help a
person escape manipulation and enslavement through pleasure and pain have
been taught by the great spiritual leaders of the East and West throughout the
centuries. Ancient Sparta was famous for training its young people to exhibit
courage in every circumstance.

   The person is seen to be a relational being, on the other hand, in that being
an agent in the world is a matter of being able to effect changes in one's
relation to it: Prince Hal's relations to his boon companions changed upon his
assuming kingship, a relationship that to him meant something much different
from anything they were able to appreciate.

ME, MYSELF, AND I

The child caught up in wonder is not reflective. This attitude of wonder is,
Aristotle says, the beginning of philosophy. It is in any case an experience of
the mystical attitude always able to be assumed by a human being,[16] an attitude that places one outside time, or in a different kind of time, perhaps the
time of *kairos* (the fitting occasion) rather than *chronos* (clock time). Medieval
writers contrasted the contemplative life of availability for mystical experience
with the active life of effective engagement with things in the world.

   Psychotherapy is at times a matter of dislodging the "me" of those who
merely receive actions from outside themselves in favor of the "I" of agency.
To become an actor in one's own life may require more modest actions than
had originally been intended. Persons who see themselves as the victims of real
or imagined injustice can remain mentally fixed upon this situation to the
detriment of their own further growth as human beings. One of the salient
features of coming to forgive those who have wronged me is that this act frees
me from the need to seek revenge, and thus strengthens my control over my
own future, the ability to set the agenda for my own life.

   The adult held thrall by pain may find himself unable to escape from re-
flecting upon his pained self: every thought and word concerns his pain and

his need to escape it. By definition, the attitude of the unreflecting child is one in which, while the child is evidently knowing, it is not at that moment attentive to itself as knower. The child in this state seems to be a pure "I" rather than a "me."[17] With the adult, getting into such a mental attitude may require a great deal of practice. It is clear that the "I" in this case is indeed a kind of asymptotic horizon, always receding, never reachable by the human mind. If one were to catch it, as it were, one would be catching not the active "I" but the "me" of reflection!

When a person focuses upon the "self" alone and one's own needs, that person can be called "selfish"; it is this "self" that the mystics try to "lose." But the disciplines engaged in to bring about this loss of self do not actually destroy but rather enhance the person, as active "maker" of one's own life.

The "self" is the object reflected upon by the acting person. The English word 'self' does not itself necessarily imply personality, but personality implies the ability to reflect upon oneself, at least in the ideal situation.

'Passion' was the word medieval philosophers commonly used for what we today call "emotion." As reactions to the impingement of objects from outside one, emotions seem less "acts" than are most actions initiated from within a person. They nevertheless serve as exceedingly fine indicators of a person's dispositions, including motives for action.

CONCLUSION

Action is another indicator of unique personality, regardless of the person's age. The mystery (rather than "problem") of pain is perhaps a kind of negative image of the mystery of the depth of human personality, and as such it gives one pause in one's rush to judge another human being. It is especially important to reverence a child's inclination to a unique personal destiny, made evident in even the infant's response to a situation.

NOTES

1. Arthur Schopenhauer, *The World as Will and Idea* (Garden City, NY: Doubleday & Company, 1961). See also Anthony Storr, "Jung's Concept of Personality," in Arthur Peacocke and Grant Gillett, eds., *Persons and Personality*, (Oxford: Basil Blackwell, 1987): "A good deal of Jung's thought seems to have been directly derived from Schopenhauer. Schopenhauer considered that individuals were the embodiment of an underlying Will which was outside space and time.... Jung took the term 'individuation' from Schopenhauer" (162–63). Patrick Gardiner, *Schopenhauer* (Baltimore: Penguin Books, Inc., 1964) says that Schopenhauer's "rooms . . . were furnished very simply, with little in the way of ornament except a statue of Buddha and a bust of Kant . . ." (21).
2. Alan Donagan, in *Choice: The Essential Element in Human Action* (New York: Routledge and Kegan Paul, 1987), reviews some of the recent literature on action

theory as it relates to the question of the importance of will in action. See 42, 155–56, and 167, for example.

3. *Aristotle's Nicomachean Ethics*, trans. H. G. Apostle (The Peripatetic Press, 1984), 9.7.1169a5–8: "... existence is to all a thing they choose and love, and we exist by being in activity; for we exist by living and *acting*." The word for *acting* here in Greek is *prattein*; Aristotle distinguishes at times between acting and making (*poiein*): the latter is in this case a subdivision of the former—artists act in many ways during their day, but at times *as maker or artist*. In the *Categories*, Aristotle devotes only a few lines to action and passion (9. 11b1–8).

4. Aristotle *Categories* 1b25–2a10; 1b25–7; *Metaphysics* 1017a24–7.

5. See Kant's *Anthropology from a Pragmatic Point of View*, trans. Mary J. Gregor (The Hague: Martinus Nijhoff, 1974), Part II, in which he discusses the person who appears, in contrast to the more strict discussion of the person as indicator of a moral law in the universe that is to be found in the *Critique of Practical Reason*, trans. Lewis White Beck (Indianapolis: Bobbs-Merrill Company, 1956), I, III. See also his *Groundwork of the Metaphysic of Morals*, trans. H. J. Paton (New York: Harper & Row, Publishers, 1964), II.

6. J. L. Austin, *How to Do Things with Words* (Cambridge: Harvard University Press, 1975); "Other Minds," *Philosophical Papers* (Oxford: Clarendon Press, 1961), 67: "But now, when I say, 'I promise,' ... I have not merely announced my intention, but, by using this formula (performing this ritual), I have bound myself to others, and staked my reputation, in a new way...."

7. "Ricoeur considers the project of linguistics which leads to structuralism and deconstruction to be misdirected inasmuch as language as discourse, the saying of something to someone, is lost."—Patrick A. Bourgeois, "Semiotics and the Deconstruction of Presence: A Ricoeurian Alternative," *The American Catholic Philosophical Quarterly*, (hereafter: ACPQ) 66, 3 (summer 1992): 361–97.

8. Thomas Aquinas, *Summa Contra Gentiles*, trans. Charles J. O'Neil (Garden City, NY: Doubleday & Company, 1957) 4, 13, 9: "action belongs to a finished and subsistent thing ... the plan of the house in the mind of the architect does not build the house; the architect builds it according to the plan." See also Thomas Aquinas, *On The Power of God*, 3 vols., trans. by the English Dominican Fathers (London: Burns Oates & Washburn, 1934), Vol. 3, q. 9, a. 2, c: "Again, it is reasonable that among individual substances the individual of a rational nature should have a special name [person], because as stated above it belongs to it properly and truly to act by itself." And, ibid., ad 2: "the term *person* denotes only a rational nature with that particular mode of existence."

9. Thomas Aquinas, *Summa Theologiae*, I, Qu. 89, 1, c.; *Contra Gentiles*, 4, 19, 2, quoting Aristotle *Nicomachean Ethics* 3.5.1114a32–b1. Karol Wojtyla has considered *The Acting Person*, trans. Andrzej Potocki (Boston: D. Reidel Publishing Co., 1979) from a phenomenological and perhaps voluntarist point of view, treating the moral activity of a fully mature human being. For Max Scheler's view of person, act, and time, see Peter Spader, "Max Scheler's Practical Ethics and the Model Person," ACPQ, 69, 1 (winter 1995): 63–81; and his "Persons, Acts and Meaning," *The New Scholasticism*, 59, 2 (spring 1985): 200–12.

10. See Aristotle *Nicomachean Ethics* 10.4 and 10.5 for his acute discussion of pleasure and pain in reference to political life, education, and the life of virtue and happiness.

11. Edith Stein, *On the Problem of Empathy*, trans. Waltraut Stein (Washington, DC: ICS Publications, 1989). On her work on the notion of human personhood, including her editing of Husserl's notes for *Ideas II*, see also Edith Stein, *Self Portrait*

in Letters, trans. Josephine Koeppel (Washington, DC: ICS Publications, 1993), nos. 5, 6, 13, 17, 19, et passim. Stein's method of arriving at the existence (or "constitution," in phenomenological language) of persons invites comparison with that of M. Merleau-Ponty and also with that of George Herbert Mead. See Mead's *Mind, Self, and Society from the Standpoint of a Social Behaviorist*, ed. and with an Introduction by Charles W. Morris (Chicago: The University of Chicago Press, 1962), 165, 172; 178: "The 'I' both calls out to the 'me' and responds to it. Taken together they constitute a personality as it appears in social experience."

12. The First Letter of Peter, 4.1.

13. Jacques Maritain's distinction between a (material) individual and a (spiritual) person, the individual subject to the state and the person ultimately above it, seems vulnerable to the objection that it subjects the individual to society in precisely the aspect of humanity that is most in need of protection from oppression by social forces. See *The Person and the Common Good*, trans. John J. Fitzgerald (New York: Charles Scribner's Sons, 1947), 60: "though the person as such is a totality, . . . the person as a material individual, is a part. Whereas the person, as person or totality, requires that the common good of the temporal society flow back over it, and even transcends the temporal society . . . yet the person still remains, as an individual or part, inferior and subordinated to the whole. . . ."

14. See P. F. Snowdon, "Persons, Animals, and Ourselves," in Christopher Gill, ed., *The Person and the Human Mind: Issues in Ancient and Modern Philosophy* (Oxford: Clarendon Press, 1990), 83–107, 91: "It has always been a serious embarrassment to Lockean, or Lockean inspired, accounts of our identity, that we think of those accidents or illnesses which disturb the normal flow of our mental life as things we live through and hence undergo."

15. *Reasons and Persons*, 273–76. Roderick Chisholm, *Person and Object*, deals with Hume, 37–41, and with Kant, 44ff. See also 213, nn. 33 and 37. On Kant's unknowable subject, see also Bernard Lonergan, *The Subject* (Milwaukee: Marquette University Press, 1968); and for a critical account of Lonergan's subject, see Eugene Webb, *Philosophers of Consciousness* (Seattle, WA: University of Washington Press, 1988), 84–90.

16. John Dewey's notion of religious experience, analogous to aesthetic experience, seems to have a large mystical component.

17. Consideration of the notion of a child's outlook on the world invites reflection upon the fact that Kant's "transcendental Ego" was the decidedly cerebral product of the mind of a man who did not rear children.

12

Persons in Time

Without a soul to do the counting, there would be no time.

—Aristotle

THE ANCIENTS ON TIME AND HUMAN BEINGS

"For time is just this: The number of a motion with respect to the prior and the posterior," Aristotle says in the *Physics*.[1] Aristotle's shorter works on natural philosophy include the treatment of subjects like memory and reminiscence, sleep and dreaming—all of which require existence in time. Even philosophers who see the human person as an enduring, subsistent being, see human existence as nonetheless essentially dynamic, and the person as a changing, evolving, growing reality. From the very beginning of human life, the person is subject to very accurately predictable and often rapid changes. But to situate the person in time is also to speak of space, for the very notion of time—of physical time, measured by the sun—depends, as Henri Bergson saw, upon that of space.[2]

Aristotle is the first philosopher to give an important role to potentiality; it constitutes an essential element in his system. But the way was prepared for this notion by Parmenides's insistence on changelessness and by Heraclitus's requirement that "All things change"; Plato's account of the world-stuff in the *Timaeus* made the need for such a concept acute. Aristotle's "first matter"[3] at once answered the need for a world-stuff and provided the purest instance of potentiality.

Analogues of this matter are to be found at every level and in every area of Aristotelian philosophy, with the exception of that of Pure Act, the already complete entelechy.[4] Most telling was Aristotle's application of the notion of potentiality to psychological questions, thereby explaining the act of sensation, the powers to sense, and that part of a living being that is "potentially alive,"[5] the "physically organized body." According to Aristotle, "the soul is the first *substance*, . . . the body is the matter, and a man or an animal, universally

119

taken, is the composite of the two. . . ."[6] The Aristotelian human being is potential to the core, a being physically composed of what can be analyzed into potential and actual principles.

It is this body-soul composition that underlies the relation between the human being and time in Aristotle's philosophy. Time, as it "measures" or "numbers" movement, is a product of the soul, not a physical reality independent of the intellect. Time itself thus becomes a pointer to the psychophysical composition of human beings. And time is important for morality which involves working for future goods.[7]

It seems that it was Plotinus who first called attention to human beings as future-oriented.[8] Grappling in his last treatise with the concept of time as a means to come to understand eternity, he makes it clear that a temporal being, "even if it is perfect, . . . in the way in which a body adequate for a soul is perfect, needs also time to come. . . ."[9] Again, "with things which have come to be, if you take away the 'will be', what happens is that they immediately cease to exist, as they are continually acquiring being. . . ."[10]

THOMAS AQUINAS ON PERSONS AND POTENCY

Thomas Aquinas's philosophy of finite beings makes clear that for him substantiality in human beings lies in the direction of potentiality,[11] thus necessarily involving temporal existence. For Thomas, the essentially temporal character of human existence is evident from the potentiality of each person's composite nature, a nature composed of potential body and actual soul which in turn is potential to its actual existence. Thus, "personality," the ultimate completion of individual human nature, is at once a perfection and a radical potentiality for the existence of each human being.

RECENT WRITERS ON THE TEMPORALITY OF PERSONS

If time is, as Aristotle claims, the "measure of motion," then the human mind is what does the measuring, and a characteristic human trait is the estimation of time. In the very act of measuring time, a human being is measured by it, becomes older, and perhaps wiser, through the discoveries time allows. In a sense, then, as Bergson shows in *Matter and Memory*,[12] the realization of the inner experience of time and its concomitant memory makes clear that the human soul is something distinct from the body, not totally "submerged" in matter as the souls of even the most knowing of other animals seem to be.

Emily Dickinson's "Forever—is composed of Nows" calls attention to those instants of wonder or any other strong emotion when one loses awareness of the passing of time, being as it were transported outside oneself like Cinderella at the ball. Such moments seem to stand outside time in the usual sense—"counted" time.[13] At such moments one is engaged in what the mystics have called "contemplation," a self-forgetful fascination with the object of one's gaze. The "loss of self" in this operation is not strictly and literally the loss of one's ontological being as a person; it is in fact usually seen by those who practice contemplation as the highest fulfillment of personal development.[14] But it is the loss of preoccupation with oneself considered as an object of attention, and, to this extent, an at least momentary loss of selfishness.

PERSONS AND THEIR HISTORIES

"When" is a category that can distinguish human beings, in a most profound way, from other earthly living beings: human beings, as the only beings on earth able to estimate time, are the only ones able to recognize that they are in time, and to reflect upon it. This characteristic of human beings has come to be called "historicity."

Only in recent centuries in the West has the notion of history taken on importance as an intellectual category. José Ortega y Gassett points out that whereas each lion is like the first lion to exist, human beings are necessarily born into an existing society with its own history and customs.[15] Not only my individual life course, then, but that of the human race is important to me as a person.

Somewhat as impinging energy disturbs very small particles in the attempt to locate them, the knower can change herself in the act of knowing herself (and thereby being known). The insight of a later act of self-knowledge is into an expanded, more differentiated self. As a result of this factorial action of self-consciousness, the word 'person' can acquire a kind of historicity analogous to that of real persons: it will undergo a change in intention as its user acquires more self-awareness. And as it undergoes changes in meaning, it can recipro-cally act upon the human being by stimulating self-awareness. If it is true that at crucial turning points in human self-reflection the notion of person will undergo change, then ignorance of or lack of advertence to some fundamental aspect of human personality can diminish human experience.

The contemporary phenomenologist Paul Brockelman points out that for human beings to act intentionally calls for a past experience on which the present is based and which opens out to the future: one needs to know what is wanting in the past in order to be able to plan now for the action one will take to bring about a future state of affairs.[16]

The marxist writer Lucien Sève has shown that the successive phases of human life can be plotted in terms of the sort of work that occupies each stage of human existence: the young person will devote a larger portion of his day to study than will the average working adult; the retired person's day will be marked by different uses of time than is the worker's. A biography, then, should ideally probe ways in which at different times of life the subject used his time.

An intellectual worker may be found to distribute his work differently over the same period of time than a factory worker, for example.[17] The theory recalls the Hindu doctrine of stages of life from that of the young person studying to that of the ascetic living withdrawn in the forest. A fruitful subject of research might be that of changing use of time by women as related to their changing self-image.

WORK AND LEISURE

Among economic considerations, in reference to time and persons, is the relation of leisure to work time.[18] As work becomes more automated, the importance of finding alternative ways of using increasingly available hours outside of work time becomes evident. How does one avoid having the world end in boredom if people are deprived of meaningful work?[19] And how does one distribute fairly the goods needed for living to the workers who produce them? Marx called attention to the relation between the capitalist economic system and the "proletariat," those workers paid just enough to be able to reproduce themselves. It would seem that cultivation of the artistic and other creative gifts of each person can alone provide a way out of the present impasse. Celebration of life and its gifts must, it seems, be given the central importance it still enjoys in some non-Western cultures.

Celebrations in these cultures emphasize not only the recurrence of the seasons like those of planting and harvest, but also certain uniquely important events: the "auspicious moment" is thus important for the performance of any act. India's Independence Day is celebrated on August 15, not on the preceding day, because it was considered by astrologers to be a day of good omen in contrast to the originally proposed August 14.

WHEN DO PERSONS BEGIN TO EXIST?

Since time has so important an influence upon the human person's existence, when can the person as such be said to begin to be? Those who see the person as identical with mind or soul must then further ask how mind or soul is related to the body. If body and mind were related only accidentally or extrinsically, then perhaps time and its influence on the person would be a matter of influence upon the body but not directly upon the soul or person. If body and soul are, as Aristotle thought, more closely related, then the manner in which time affects the soul or mind through the body is a subject that needs further study.

For those who see the mind as the person, the person might be said to begin when the human individual gives evidence of mental activity. Or, if one takes the mind to be eternal, then the person would be as eternal as the mind, perhaps going through many successive incarnations in a variety of bodies, human or otherwise.

For those who see the person as essentially a substance, the question of when a person can be said to begin to be will involve that of the time at which this individual substance can be said to have begun; for those who see persons as constituted by relationships, the essentially constituting relation will mark the beginning of a person's existence. Is this relationship that of the person with his or her parents? Does it depend upon the larger society? Or is one, in fact, a person when so recognized in law?

In either case, whether it is relation or substantiality or some combination of the two that can best be said to constitute personhood, the person's distinctive acts will indicate personhood. But which are my distinctive acts? Is it my finger- or voiceprints that distinctively identify me? Is it possession of my individual genes, genes that may make me in some way incompatible with my mother in the womb? Or, for my distinctive acts, must society wait until I have distinguished myself by making a useful invention or scientific discovery, or by creating a striking work of art, or perhaps by rearing children so that they can become responsible adults?

If the human person is integrally body and soul, then must one say that human personality begins at a definite point in time, say at conception or at implantation? If the body must be adequate to the needs of the informing soul, at what stage in human development can this be said to be the case? Certainly it would seem that everything that will be used by the adult is present in at least a potential state in the newly penetrated ovum. Will this explosively developing individual proceed in a direct way to the complete realization of its finished adult state? Or will it proceed in stages, with a kind of leap from one to the next, like a butterfly from a cocoon? And in this case will the leap represent the relinquishment of one form's influence upon the developing fetus to that of a successive form or soul?

A famous discussion in the Middle Ages concerned the number of forms in a living thing: Would a person, for example, have a vegetative, an animal, and a spiritual soul coexisting in him or her at the present time? And if so, how would these be related and how would they interact? Thomas Aquinas held that in a human being vegetative, animal, and rational forms were present successively: the vegetative soul controlled the first days or weeks of the developing embryo, to be succeeded at the appropriate time by an animal soul, that took over its vegetative functions in addition to providing distinctively animal functions to the developing fetus.[20] The Franciscan doctors preferred the theory of many simultaneously existing forms in one human being.

In either case, one is left with the question of when one can be said to be a "person." Should one say that everything needed for adult human life is present from the beginning, although in a potential state? Or ought one say that it is only at the time of actual infusion of the "rational" soul (perhaps as long as forty days into the pregnancy) that one can be said to be this distinctive human person? Much depends upon whether personhood is identified with potentiality or with actuality.

William A. Wallace calls attention to a theory of intermediate forms, forms that, for example, might be said to replace the defunct soul of a just-dead animal.[21] The ultimate resolution of the dead body into various chemical elements will take time. In the meantime, these intermediate forms would preside over the orderly decomposition of the body through its various intermediate states. One would have to know when the human soul was replaced by such an intermediate form in order to identify the exact point of death. Some thinkers try to identify similar stages of coming-to-be in reference to the new person coming into being.

Derek Parfit distinguishes a "human being" from a "person" and believes that a person is more like a nation than like a physical individual. These assumptions permit him to assert a gradual change from a human embryo to a human person; he concludes that:

> We can now deny that a fertilized ovum is a person or a human being. This is like the plausible denial that an acorn is an oak-tree.[22]

And, with reference to death, he thinks that:

> If we know that the human being is in a coma that is incurable . . . we shall believe that the person has ceased to exist. Since there is a living human body, . . . the human being still exists.[23]

Contrary to the proverb, however, it seems that nature does proceed by leaps, and although it may not be possible to get agreement upon the question of just when the developing tree should be called an oak, there *is* a definite point at which it has reached that stage, though we may not yet be able to detect that point. What we say about persons reflects a conscious choice as to whether we acknowledge their being or not.

CONCLUSION

None of the categories is more revealing of the person than that of time. The body is essentially involved in time; the mind not only "counts" (apparently usually at a level below that of focal consciousness) but is itself evidently affected by the passage of time: it is possible today to appreciate the reciprocal influence of computers on those who use them, a realization not generally possible fifty years ago. Historicity characterizes even the most abstract ideas, since the universe of discourse in which words are used changes over the years. It seems evident that to understand any human person it is necessary to take account of that individual's position in time, from every point of view: the stage of world history at which one is born, the intellectual climate then prevailing, and the use the person decides to make of the time allotted to him or her.

NOTES

1. Aristotle *Physics* 4.11.219b2–4 (H. G. Apostle trans). See also 4.14.223a25–28.
2. Bergson's doctoral thesis (Paris, 1889) dealt with Aristotle's notion of place.
3. Aristotle *Physics* 1.9.
4. Aristotle *Metaphysics* 9.3.1947a30; 12.6.1072b28.
5. Aristotle *De Anima* 2.1.412a20–21; 412b4–6.
6. Aristotle *Metaphysics* (H. G. Apostle trans.) (Z), 7.11.1037a5–7.
7. See G. Verbeke, "Moral Behaviour and Time in Aristotle's Nicomachean Ethics," *Kephalaion: Studies in Greek Philosophy and its Continuation offered to Professor C. J. De Vogel* (Assen, The Netherlands: Van Gorcum & Comp., B. V., 1975), 78–90.
8. Plotinus, *Enneads*, trans. A. J. Armstrong, The Loeb Classical Library, 6 vols. (Cambridge, MA: Harvard University Press, 1980), III, 3, 7, "On Eternity and Time."
9. *Enneads* III, 7. 6. 38–42. See Gerard J. P. O'Daly, *Plotinus' Philosophy of the Self*, (New York: Barnes and Noble Books, 1973) 15, 18, 20–21, 27, 60, and 89.
10. Plotinus, *Enneads* III, 7. 4. 10–19. Plotinus also distinguished the soul from what he called "we," which might be called the ego. See the comments on the chapter by H.-R. Schwyzer, "'Bewusst' und 'Unbewusst' bei Plotin," in E. R. Dodds, et al., ed., *Les Sources de Plotin* (Geneve: Fondation Hardt, 1960), 385.
11. *Summa Theologiae*, I, Qu. 3, 2–3. For a contemporary investigation of the temporal character of persons, see R. Chisholm, *Person and Object* (La Salle, IL: Open Court Publishing Co., 1976), 136–7: "Our definition has the consequence that, if an individual thing x is a person, then, in every possible world in which x exists, x is a person from the moment it comes into being until the moment it passes away." See also 98ff.
12. Henri Bergson, *Matter and Memory* (Paris, 1896; New York: G. Allen & Co., 1921), distinguishes between clock time, which is in a sense spatial: (think of the movement of the sun across the sky), and the experience of time not tied to spatial measures, the latter, perhaps, what we experience when we say that time stands still.
13. Bergson contrasts the time of the physical sciences with what he calls "*durée*," this momentary subsumption into the supertemporal world.
14. See, for example, Flannery O'Connor, *The Habit of Being*, ed. Sally Fitzgerald (New York: Random House, 1980), 136: "I guess meditation and contemplation and all the ways of prayer boil down to keeping it firmly in sight that there are two." Also, 458: "Writing is a great example of self-abandonment. I never completely forget myself except when I am writing. It is the same with Christian self-abandonment. The great difference between Christianity and the Eastern religions is the Christian insistence on the fulfillment of the individual person . . ."
15. José Ortega y Gassett, *Obras*, VI, 40–43, "History as System," cited in Julián Marías, *History of Philosophy*, trans. Stanley Appelbaum and Clarence C. Strowbridge (New York: Dover Publications, 1967), 458–62. See also Marías's "The Experience of Life," 279–307 in *Philosophy as Dramatic Theory* (University Park, PA: The Pennsylvania State University Press, 1971).
16. Paul Brockelman, *Time and Self: Phenomenological Explorations* (New York: The Crossroad Publishing Company and Scholars Press, 1985), 31: "a present situation must be seen in the context of an horizon of retentions and anticipations." Values, as Max Scheler established, finally underly human actions. See also 21–25 et passim, and Martin Heidegger, *Being and Time*, on Dasein as "being toward death";

and, on Heidegger's *Dasein*, Frederick A. Olafson, "Consciousness and Intention-ality in Heidegger's thought," *American Philosophical Quarterly*, 12, 2 (April 1975): 99: "as though *Dasein* were a fragment broken off from the transcendental ego . . . attached to a particular . . . time and space."

17. Lucien Sève, *Marxisme et Théorie de la Personnalité*, 4è éd, (Paris: Editions sociales, 1975), 208, 244 et passim. On the possibility of work being demeaning, see Robert Paul Wolff, "There's Nobody Here But Us Persons," 128–44 in Carol G. Gould, ed., *Women and Philosophy* (New York: G. P. Putnam's Sons, 1976).

18. See Josef Pieper's classic, *Leisure: the Basis of Culture*, trans. Alexander Dru (New York: Pantheon Books, [1952]. He finds that "cult," or religious observance, is at the basis of culture.

19. This is a recurrent theme in the writings of P. Teilhard de Chardin. See his "Some Reflections on the Spiritual Repercussions of the Atom Bomb," Chap. VIII, in *The Future of Man* (New York: Harper & Row, 1969), 150.

20. See Thomas Aquinas, *The Literal Exposition on Job* (Atlanta: The Scholars Press, 1989), On 21, 3–13, p. 283 [21, 1].

21. William A. Wallace, "Nature and Human Nature as Norm in Medical Ethics," in *Catholic Perspectives on Medical Morals: Foundational Issues*, ed. E. D. Pellegrino et al., *Philosophy and Medicine* Series, Vol. 34 (Boston: D. Reidel Publishing Co., 1989). Wallace's view is discussed in Philip Smith's, "Transient Natures at the Edges of Life: A Thomistic Exploration," *The Thomist*, 54 (1990): 191–227; see also Thomas Aquinas, *Disputed Questions on the Power of God*, III, 9–11.

22. Derek Parfit, *Reasons and Persons* (Oxford: Oxford University Press, 1984), 322.

23. *Reasons and Persons*, 323. Here Parfit is following Locke's distinction between per-son and human being.

13

The Category of "Having" as Revealing the Person

It seems that clothes symbolize in the human mind certain magical powers, hence to be without them is to be "utterly powerless" as Freud puts it.

—Jyoti Sahi

CLOTHING AND ITS IMPORTANCE

John Stuart Mill considered "having" or "habit" (first of all in the sense of clothing: a riding habit, for example) too trivial to rank as one of the categories. It is, nonetheless, particularly revealing of the nature of the human person. This is so because clothes (and possessions in general) are needed by human beings for their various activities. This is the subject of discussion in the present chapter.[1]

Funeral customs offer striking examples of the significance of clothing and other possessions. Archeologists recognize that burial customs reflect the social position of the deceased as well as physical and spiritual aspects of the society. Funeral customs represent an attempt to ensure that the relationships between the dead person and those still living will endure in some meaningful way. The perdurance of funeral customs over millenia bears witness to the profound emotional significance of the death of a human being.

This is shown in the clothing in which a person is buried, or the things buried with the body of the deceased. The warrior's spear, no longer needed for battles in this life, is perceived as possibly useful in the next world. A baby's favorite toy, a woman's jewelry—whatever has come to be seen as inseparable from that person—may be lovingly separated from ordinary use and given a kind of consecration by being buried with the person's body. Desecration of a cemetery is generally considered an attack upon the whole society, seen as having historical reality.

Clothing is a symbol as well as a protection. Whether the person being honored in death is a pharaoh or an ordinary infant, recognition of the person as such is here obviously displayed: not every dead body is that of King Tut; the long-awaited and untimely lost infant, however, will be treasured even in death.

The objects buried with a person's body belong to the category of habit, or in a more general sense, possession.[2] Studying the predicates assigned to this category can provide numerous insights not only into the nature of personality, but also into the individual human person.

ARISTOTLE ON POSSESSIONS

Aristotle has much to say about possessions, notably that they are necessary for human beings, who, when they regard property as their own, get "immense pleasure" from this, because it is "natural and not in vain for each man to love himself"[3] and because property enables one to be generous to others and thus practice virtue.

As Aristotle makes clear in his *Categories* and elsewhere, the Greek word for "to have" is not a univocal term; rather, it has many meanings.[4] One can be said to have qualities or quantities, or a certain form; Atlas "holds" the earth; the container "has" the contained. What "holds" things together as a continuum is another example of the use of this term. One has property, the parts of one's body, even a wife or husband.

Aristotle lists the categories somewhat differently in his various works, depending upon the intention he has in each: *Metaphysics* deals with being, *Topics* with argument, and *Physics* with bodies in regard to motion. In the book of definitions in the *Metaphysics*, he says that "having is a kind of act (*energeia*) of the one having and the thing had . . . as between the one who has a garment and the garment which is had."[5] One treats what one has according to one's own nature or desire, which is why "fever is said to hold a man, or a tyrant, a city." Thus when we are clothed, we "have on" or wear our clothes.

Of all these meanings, however, it is the last that he uses to instantiate habit in the *Categories*: "of possessing, 'is shod' and 'is armed'; . . ."[6] This is the third sense in the list of nonunivocal senses in the last chapter of the *Categories*: " . . . something he wears, such as a coat or a tunic, or something he wears on a part of the body, such as a ring on the hand; . . ."[7]

The list of Aristotle's senses of what may be called the peculiar meaning of 'habit' (as distinct from that which it may share with another category such as quality) is, then:

> is shod
> is armed
> wears a coat or tunic
> wears a ring.

Each of these predicates speaks not only about the nature of the one thus described, but also about the individual him- or herself, as will become clear from a consideration of each item in turn.

To be shod is important in a country like Greece, with its wide variations in temperature and its mountainous terrain. Footgear can identify a group of people: jogging shoes are different from tennis shoes or mountaineers' boots, and each is appropriate to a particular activity. Ideally, a shoe takes on the form of the individual foot. And within the range of possible decorations of shoes, individual persons can choose the style pleasing to themselves. Animals can be shod, as horses are, but only by human beings, and for human purposes.

Making and using arms—or, more broadly, any tool—can be said to belong to human nature; it is also something that can be chosen by a human being. Other animals, and even plants, can be said to be armed, but the word is then used somewhat differently, since human armaments (even those put on horses, for example, in the Middle Ages) are artificial means of defense, while those of animals are naturally given.

Important developments in art and technology in the course of time take place because the artist or workman has found or invented a new tool. "It is a poor workman who blames his own tools," because a good workman's first concern is to provide himself with appropriate tools for the job at hand.[8]

CLOTHES MAKE THE MAN

To wear clothes is at once proper to human nature (as contrasted with animal natures), and also characteristic of each human being. A person's choice of clothing enables one to be identified as a particular individual, and also as part of a special group. Successful business and professional men and women are encouraged to choose "power suits"; those who belong to various social movements may wear T-shirts to identify them as members. The Nazi strategy of reducing their victims to nakedness was part of a calculated attempt to depersonalize them.[9]

Negatively, clothing tells something about the individuality of persons. Proverbially, "The habit does not make the monk": more is required than merely a change of clothing to make one a spiritual person—or a competent doctor or a skilled welder. The whole question of the relation of clothing to holiness (like that of the relation between person and symbol) invites further reflection.[10]

THOMAS AQUINAS ON HAVING

Thomas Aquinas points out that there is a connection between "having" and activity: "*Having* (*possession* or *habit*) means in one sense a certain activity of the haver and of the thing had, as a sort of action or motion."[11] Aristotle also says: "To have [or 'possess', or 'hold'] has many meanings. (1) To treat according to one's own nature o[r] tendency; accordingly, fever is said to possess the man, the tyrants are said to have cities, and wearers of clothes to have the clothes."[12] On this, Thomas Aquinas comments: "Then he gives four ways in which the term *to have* (to possess or hold) is used. First, to have a thing is to treat it according to one's own nature in the case of natural things, or according to one's own impulse in the case of voluntary matters."[13]

Thomas explains that a person putting on clothing is, as it were, acting, just as making is the action of the maker on the made, which receives the action. Thus clothing is measured to the wearer, so that it takes on that person's characteristics, and ultimately it expresses the choice, the will, of the wearer, as well as that person's bodily impressions. " . . . because clothing is fitted to the one who wears it and so it takes on his figure."[14] Eyeglasses or a cane are fitted to the individual.

JEWELRY

Finally, a person may wear jewelry and this may be the most personal type of "habit." Even a member of an equatorial tribe otherwise naked will wear bracelets, necklaces, and finger, nose, or earrings. Some of these ornaments are, as I was told in India, related in some way to acupressure. In any case they can indicate a great deal about the status and the individual taste of the wearer.

Jewelry can indicate a person's age or marital status, wealth, or a certain office or position of authority. Jewelry can have powerful symbolic and emotional meaning and therefore may be treated ritually: a piece of jewelry may be passed down through generations in a family; a wedding ring may be buried with a person. A signet ring is broken when its owner dies.

Animals may display ornaments—a decorated harness, gilt horns, bells, embellished collars—but these are put on by human beings, often precisely to indicate wealth or ownership by someone.

CLOTHING AND THE BODY AS A SYSTEM OF MEANINGS

The Indian anthropologist Veena Das criticizes what may be called a quasi-Cartesian distinction made by Victor Turner and others between bodily experiences—and phenomena "supposedly 'given' in nature,"—and, on the other hand, "ethical principles and values" lacking this givenness. This distinction is unfortunate since it assumes that the

> body is something given in nature and its experience is universally shared; that the experiences of the body are concrete rather than abstract; and that the body in consequence can be described and made the object of conative and affective aspects of experience alone. It is those experiences that are given priority over the body as a culturally cognizable object.[15]

She prefers to see the body as a "system of meanings," as a "culturally created" symbol rather than merely a "biological substance." Similarly, both clothing and nudity function as symbols: the person who "goes around naked or dresses himself with . . . bark, leaves, or skins of wild animals, fasting, living on fruits and leaves, ... is, in cultural terms, an asocial being."[16] Das here echoes statements of Aristotle and Thomas about the dynamic, willed character of human dress and the reflection it provides of the human spirit. The contemporary Indian student of symbol, Jyoti Sahi, also observes that the Indian holy man's nakedness symbolizes both his detachment and also an erotic quality. The Buddhist monk is to wear clothes that are patched and thus look "like a ploughed field."

G. M. Hopkins's "gear, tackle, and trim," everything human beings need to live and work, is what Aristotle understands as belonging to "habit." Keys, pens, paper, a particular sort of screwdriver or wrench, these objects make easy or in some cases even make possible human creative work. Possession and access to possessions can mean the difference between life and death for a human person. The ultimate attempt to deny personality, as Kant saw, is making a person a mere means to an end, a tool.[17] Hegel's picture of the dialectic of master and slave also points to the importance of tools as means to work and to develop one's personality creatively in such a way as to become free oneself and to free others, even oppressors.[18]

Animals that mark a certain piece of ground as belonging to them exhibit "territoriality," but they do not set up empires, as human beings may. Human beings choose to exert or accept authority on a scale unknowable to other animals.

SOME SOCIAL, ECONOMIC, AND MORAL IMPLICATIONS OF HAVING

How much property should a person have? " ... as much as will make a man lead a temperate and generous life," because "temperance and generosity are the virtues which must make use of [material goods]."[19]

Succeeding eras of fashion in clothing tell something about the history of a society. The history of workers' relations to their tools remains incomplete, if only because the effects of the information revolution upon society are as yet incompletely understood. In technologically advanced societies today computers and robots are replacing workers; women and men who had prepared themselves for lifetime employment in a particular field may find that, after they have lost a job, it is highly unlikely that they will ever be hired in that field again.

If the workforce can be divided into those who produce goods and services that are immediately marketable and those who create principally for the sake of the joy that creation gives them—artists—it seems that it is the first group with whom economic laws deal for the most part. They are said to be employed or not and to have or lack the means to buy what they need. With changes in the world economic situation, these workers can change from contributing members of society to an impoverished proletariat.

It is no doubt important, then, for every person to be educated from as early an age as possible to realize the creative side of his or her personality so as to be able to make and do what is fulfilling to them and to the eventual benefit of society. Also social provision must be made for the support of the arts.[20] With the breakup of much of the Communist world, the time is probably at hand for working out a new order combining the best features of socialist and capitalist modes of possession.

CONCLUSION: HABIT THE MOST PERSONAL CATEGORY

From what has been said it can be seen that habit is perhaps the most human and most personal category, inasmuch as clothing, decoration, and tools do not seem to have much to do with divine or angelic or animal beings, but solely with human persons, as such.

It is as a bodily being that a person needs possessions, and it is because human beings, having intellect, can foresee the need for possessions that they are able to provide for themselves adequately. A worker needs to know where his or her tools are, to have them at hand, in order to work efficiently.[21] But possession is always a social act: to "own" something would seem to be meaningless if there were no other person able to lay claim to what I possess.[22] A person alone on the planet would possess all—and none—of it: possession has meaning only relative to others. The naked ascetic who begs all his food serves as a focus for the community to which he belongs. Because he must beg for his food and his other needs, he is the living exemplification of the relatedness of persons to one another. Possession, or its deliberate renunciation, thus shows persons as related beings in the very act of owning or claiming for themselves what they need to live and work.

Clothing and other possessions are needed by human beings, whatever be the mode of possession, because they enable a person to fit into his or her place. Fitting into a place is difficult because of both the place and the individual. A man seven feet tall, for example, may need to have a special bed. One person may wear out more pairs of shoes, another more shirts. A tropical forest dweller set down in Alaska would die of cold without proper clothing. Astronauts need special clothing to fit them into their extraordinary environment. Possessions are a feature of each person as person, because one person's needs are different from those of another, and to meet these needs requires special gear peculiar to that individual. There exists a society to facilitate exchange of shoes among persons who need different sizes of shoes on their left and right feet.

An infant depends upon others to provide for his or her needs, as does a person too old to work. To deprive someone of the possessions he or she needs in order to develop is to stunt that person's growth. Clothing, and possessions in general, indicate a great deal about the person who has them. Thus, this category is, in a sense, the most human of all, and symbolically the most revealing of the individual person.

NOTES

1. The word 'habit' in the sense of the category under discussion here is to be distinguished from the more commonly used 'habit' that is a quality: in the latter sense, smoking can be called a habit, a way of behaving that has become usual as a result of one or more acts of smoking. In this latter sense, of habitual action, habit is a kind of quality. The word 'habit' is still taken in English to mean clothing in the case of a monk's "habit" or distinctive clothing.

2. "Nicostratus, ap. Simpl. 368.12ff., criticises Aristotle for not providing a discussion of the category *echein* [to have] which would include all the uses of that word enumerated in the 'Postpraedicamenta' (15 b 17ff.)."—H. B. Gottshalk, "Aristotelian Philosophy in the Roman World from the Time of Cicero to the End of the Second Century A.D.," *ANRW* 36:2, p. 1151, n. 345. Kant criticized Aristotle for adding to the categories the postpredicaments "some of which . . . are contained in the former. . . ."—*Prolegomena to Any Future Metaphysics*, trans. Lewis White Beck (New York: Liberal Arts Press, [1950]), 70. Thomas Aquinas considers "having" from a metaphysical point of view in his *Commentary on Aristotle's Metaphysics* (hereafter: *In Met.*), trans. John P. Rowan (Chicago: Henry Regnery Co., 1961) 1062ff.

3. Aristotle *Politics* trans. H. G. Apostle, 2.5.1263b.

4. Aristotle *Categories* 15.15b18–34; see also *Topics*, in *Aristotle Selected Works*, trans. H. G. Apostle and Lloyd P. Gerson (Grinnell, IA: The Peripatetic Press, 1982), 1.9.103b22–36; and *Aristotle's Physics*, trans. H. G. Apostle (Grinnell, IA: The Peripatetic Press, 1969), 3.1.200b.28–201a.8–25.

5. Aristotle *Metaphysics* 5.20.1022b4–14; 1023a8–25.

6. Aristotle *Categories* 2a3.

7. Aristotle *Categories* 15b21–24.

8. The logical works of Aristotle constitute his "organon" or tool.

9 See *Edith Stein: Self-Portrait in Letters*, trans. Josephine Koeppel (Washington, DC: Institute of Carmelite Studies, 1993), 353. Stein, a Jewish philosopher who became a Carmelite nun, was arrested by the Nazis in retaliation for the protest of the Dutch bishops against Nazi atrocities. A few days before her death she sent word from the concentration camp that she needed a veil.

10. Sahi, *The Child and the Serpent* (London: Routledge and Kegan Paul, 1980) 53–4. Sahi also remarks that the "feminine . . . is clothed in space (digambara)." 'Digambara' refers at times to nakedness. Is this a statement about the powerlessness of women in Indian society?

11. Thomas Aquinas, *In Met.* trans. John P. Rowan (Chicago: Henry Regnery Co., 1961), 5 (509), commenting on *Metaphysics* 5.1023a8ff. See also Aristotle's contrasting of action as "in progress" with having: *Ethics* 9.9.1169b29.

12. Aristotle *Metaphysics* (delta), 5.1023a9–11.

13. Thomas Aquinas, *In Met.*, 1080.

14. *Ibid.*, 1080, 1062.

15. Veena Das, "Paradigms of Body Symbolism: An Analysis of Selected Themes in

Hindu Culture," in Richard Burghart and Audrey Cantile, eds., *Indian Religion* (New York: St. Martin's Press, 1985), 180–181.

16. *Ibid.*, 193.

17. Immanuel Kant, *Groundwork of the Metaphysic of Morals*, trans. H. J. Paton (New York: Harper & Row, 1964), Chapter II, 106–07: ". . . every rational being, as an end in himself, must be able to regard himself as also the maker of universal law in respect of any law whatever to which he may be subjected; for it is precisely the fitness of his maxims to make universal law that marks him out as an end in himself. . . . this dignity . . . carries with it the necessity of always choosing his maxims from the point of view of himself—and also of every other rational being—as a maker of law (and this is why they are called persons)."

18. G. W. F. Hegel, *The Phenomenology of Mind*, trans. J. B. Baillie, (New York: Harper & Row, 1977), B, IV, A, 229–40.

19. Aristotle *Politics* 2.6.1265a33–38.

20. See Dewey's discussion of art and other work in *Reconstruction in Philosophy*, Chap. VIII, 211: "Making a living economically speaking, will be at one with making a life that is worth living [in a society that liberates human capacities]."

21. See Martin Heidegger, *Being and Time*, trans. John Macquarrie and Edward Robinson (New York: Harper & Row, 1962) for his discussion of the meaning of tools.

22. On the importance of "owning" for the person from a marxist point of view, see John R. Wikse, *About Possession: The Self as Private Property* (University Park, PA: Pennsylvania State University Press, 1977).

Conclusion

The word 'person' has been given different emphases in different times, partly because of the various cultural contexts in which the term was being used. In the theological climate in which Boethius offered his original definition of the word, a kind of "genus" of persons included God, angels, and human beings. When Locke elaborated his definition of the word a millenium later, he apparently had Boethius's sorts of persons in mind. In trying to set forth a definition applicable to all of them, however, he made the human person a more cerebral and certainly a less materially substantial being than Boethius had. In this way he helped set the stage for the sorts of Cartesian understandings of the person found in much philosophical discussion today.

PERSONS: STRUCTURE AND FUNCTION

Even today, the meaning of the word 'person' is affected by two distinct emphases originating in the ancient Greek and Latin languages: a "functional" connotation, with a legal emphasis, associated with the Latin source of the word, *persona*, and a more physical, "structural" emphasis, associated with the Greek, *prosopon*.

The tradition stemming from the Greek sees human persons as primarily bodily beings (who can also be given legal standing) and tends to emphasize such qualities of human persons as their capacity for future development. Persons are seen in this understanding as essentially beings full of promise.

Heirs of the Latin legal sense of the word, on the other hand, include corporate persons, their status established by law, and also those who, like John Dewey, favor a prescriptive rather than a descriptive definition of 'person', giving personhood the status of an achievement.

John Dewey appreciated the central position of the human person as citizen; he looked for the classical antecedent of 'person' in the Latin *persona* (ignoring the Greek); and he inferred that personhood is essentially a matter of agency, not substantiality, and that one becomes a person in being socialized. In this Dewey echoes the interests and usage of Hobbes and Locke. Although the latter thinkers were aware of the Greek tradition, their systematic interests gave them reason to emphasize the political position of the person, and this in turn made the connotations of the Latin *persona* useful to them.

STRUCTURE OF PERSONS

The Aristotelian categories, in particular those of substance, relation, and action, have been used to analyze the structure of the human person. Those theologians and philosophers who find the categories too "natural" (and so, impersonal) criticize their use in reference to persons. Their objections, however, often on completely extraneous grounds, show these critics to be unacquainted with the true meaning of the categories.

The structural view takes the person as physically given and attempts to describe in what the person's personhood consists. The functional view, on the other hand, tends to prescribe the requirements for personhood: being male, free, of a certain nation or race, property owner, and so on.

Those who attempt to uncover the structure of human personality may use the category of substance, as Boethius did, or may see relation or action as fundamental. All three categories—relation, act, and substance—help one understand the nature of human personality: substance, by making clear that a person exists in that person's own right, "*per se*"; relation, by affirming that no human person could exist unrelated; and action, by making explicit the temporal character of human existence: human persons attain their perfection by acting.

Thomas Aquinas, using the works of classical and patristic thinkers as well as those of Moslem and Jewish teachers, explained the human person as a substantial being composed of a body and soul potential to the existence proper to each person.

Richard of Saint Victor and John Duns Scotus, each in his own way, made clear the importance of relation to the human person. Phenomenologists, notably Gabriel Marcel, have enriched our notions of person by emphasizing the importance of the person as a related being, a person called and fated to act. Scheler speaks of "act-substance" in reference to the person, while K. Wojtyla refers to the "act-person."

During the nineteenth century, under the influence of J. S. Mill and others, the notion of the person as a substantial being, in the sense of Boethius's definition, was gradually lost. Philosophical discussions since that time have dealt more often with the question of personal identity, a question introduced by Locke, than with the meaning of 'person' itself.

PERSON AND THE TRANSCENDENTALS

Although the categories clarify important aspects of human life, "there are more things in heaven and earth" than can be put into categories. Some predicates, like the word 'being', seem to "overflow" the bounds of the categories, since they are found in every one of them; and these notions are perhaps supremely important for the actual lives of human beings.

Something has been said already about the nature of relationship. Augustine, in the fifth century, pointed out that the idea of relation was not confined in its use to an accidental meaning. It could, in suitable circumstances, apply to substance as well as accident. In the language of later medieval thinkers, it could be called "transcendental": it is a predicate not able to be confined to one category. Examples of transcendental predicates, besides "being"—which is predicable not only of substance but of each accident—are "one," "true," and "good." These notions "overflow," as it were, the limits of the classifications that the categories provide. These transcendental attributes of being— reality, oneness, distinction, truth, goodness, and beauty—can lead one to a deeper understanding of what it means to be a person than would be possible without them.

The attribute of oneness encourages reflection on the importance of the process of integration and of the dimensions and ingredients of integrity. The transcendental attribute of beauty challenges not only the philosopher or logician, but anyone who reflects upon the experience of meeting a beautiful or a less than obviously beautiful human being. Goodness follows being in such a way that no human being can ever be completely bad. Discussion about the importance of "quality of life" tends to emphasize the good; those who argue for the even greater value of life itself are persuaded by their insight into the fundamental importance of being.

The study of these transcendental attributes of being, however, belongs properly not to logic or natural philosophy, but to metaphysics—the part of philosophy that treats of being *itself* rather than the particular human form of being and the logic able to deal with it. And so, because the primary focus of this work is natural and logical, these attributes are not taken up here.

What the preceding discussion has shown is that each of the categories, those of time and place as well as position, possessions, and receiving, of quantity and especially that of quality—of the rational mind, for example—each has its particular light to cast upon the reality of human personality. These categories, like those of substance, action, and relation, remind us to ask questions about the nature of human persons, and to listen for answers not only in our own Western culture, but wherever human persons are to be found.

Appendix: Personalisms

Within the present century schools of philosophy dealing with the person developed, largely independently of one another, in France and in the United States. "Boston Personalism" (with adherents in Los Angeles and other places) has emphasized chiefly the human person as a spiritual being, and the divine as personal, while the French personalist school has tended to deal with social issues involving persons, like the ability of a woman to hold property. These thinkers have considered such classical questions of philosophy as the relation between body and soul in light of a commitment to the preeminent importance of the person, divine or human.

The concerns of these "personalist" philosophers are mostly beside the point of the present work, since its emphasis has been upon a logical and natural approach to the study of the human person. A brief look at some of the thinkers involved in each will however show where some of the threads traced in the present work intersect with those woven by earlier thinkers.

NÉDONCELLE ON FRENCH PERSONALISM

In his book, *Toward a Philosophy of Love and of the Person*,[1] Maurice Nédoncelle discusses the continuity as well as the limits of human consciousness and communication and offers a survey of the history of personalism. In the survey he identifies the beginnings of the use of 'personalism':

> The word is recent in philosophy. It seems to have come from Germany, where the commentaries of Spinoza brought it forth in the context of . . . the question of knowing whether the idea of an infinite personality was acceptable. When in 1798 Herder spoke of God as 'impersonal Being,' his opponents [became known as] . . . personalists . . . [Schleiermacher, Jacobi]. In England . . . the first philosophical use of the word occurred in 1865. . . .
> . . . Renouvier succeeded in popularizing 'personalism', ridding it of pejorative connotations [*Personalism*, 1903].[2]

Other names associated with the development of personalism include those of W. Stern, B. P. Bowne, Max Scheler, N. Berdiaev, and R. T. Flewelling.

Laberthonnière in his posthumously published work and Emmanuel Mounier in the periodical *Esprit* promoted the cause of a "personalist and communitarian" revolution in France. J. Lacroix, P. Ricoeur, L. Lavelle, and such other thinkers as Le Senne, Marcel, and Maritain put forward the personalist agenda, from a variety of points of view.[3]

139

From the perspective of the present work, it can be noted that Nédoncelle sees as primary the task of rethinking the categories devised for classifying objects in view of making them applicable to subjects.[4] The category of "having" for example helps persons see themselves as limited.

> As long as there are philosophers, there will be talk of cause, of substance, of end. But these discredited notions . . . need to be rethought. Meditation on the person and on the link between persons urges more than anything else such reconsideration.

Nédoncelle discusses the social relations of the person, noting that one's physical situation—close or distant—(one's place, to use Aristotle's term), has a bearing upon one's interaction with a group.

Again, "human beings have invented a prodigiously subtle form of mask, language. Clothing and language detach themselves from us, while natural expression remains attached to the body. . . ."[5]

"A work of art, surely, is an ontic center, a quasi-person, virtually independent of its creator as an infant is of its parents . . ." for Nédoncelle.[6] And, "a fact altogether foreseeable: the fact that no epoque can offer to all the arts an equally fertile field."[7] It is clear that three of Aristotle's categories are mentioned here, clothing, place, and time.

WALTER MUELDER'S EMBODIED AND EMBEDDED PERSON

The monumental work of Borden Parker Bowne, at the beginning of the twentieth century, in the United States, brought the notion of person to the center of philosophical debate. Bowne was a man of vast erudition and of considerable stature among philosophers and theologians. As the head of the philosophy department at Boston University for many years, he formed numerous young divinity and philosophy students and made possible the development of a school of philosophers that flourished for decades both in Boston and in Los Angeles.

In the periodical, *The Personalist,* published in Los Angeles, the group's ideas were carried to the scholarly world, while in Boston University became a center of ferment for all who were interested in the development of human personality.

Among Bowne's followers, outstanding in this endeavor, were A. C. Knudson, Peter Bertocci, and the long-time Dean of Boston University's School of Theology, Walter Muelder. While each of these thinkers emphasized a distinct aspect of personalism (Muelder, i.e., identified Marxist views that favored the notion of personalism), they agreed on some fundamental theses: that human persons have a spiritual component, a soul with an immortal destiny, and that God, however envisioned, is a personal being. While the Boethian definition is cited in Bowne's masterful work, however, it is rarely referred to by later members of the group, who preferred a spiritual emphasis amid the growing materialism and behaviorism of the century.

In a paper read in December 1994 at the meeting of the Personalist Discussion Group, Dean Muelder presented his reflections on the outstanding representatives of the movement known as Boston Personalism, making clear the importance of the human person as an embodied being and as a being embedded in society. Muelder defines a person as "an experient (a self) capable of reasoning and willing ideal values."[8]

For Edgar S. Brightman, according to Muelder, "physical nature is in God, but there is . . . no analogous inclusion of any aspect of nature in the human person."[9] What Muelder calls "organic pluralism" conveys the notion that while persons, human and divine, constitute a society, there is an organic wholeness to this world of persons that has a common base in a divine creative source. For Brightman, persons are "a temporal flow of 'shining presents'" interacting with "'illuminating absents.'"[10] For J. H. Lavely, mind-body is an ontological whole.[11]

Persons have in this view "basic traits such as temporality with time-transcendence . . . awareness of space and space-transcendence . . ." and " . . . persons not only have experience, they *are* their experiences. . . ."[12] At the opposite pole from panpsychism, Knudson, Brightman, Bertocci, Lavely and other personalists hold that there is interaction between mind and body, and Muelder argues for expanding this to include society.[13]

Dean Robert C. Neville and others use a Platonic and a process philosophy approach to their studies of the person. "Minds, bodies, nature and culture interact and they have common components like time, activity, purpose and value."[14] "For Brightman, the Pattern and Receptacle [of the *Timaeus*] are both in God."[15] For Neville, "Understanding the nature of particular things is primarily understanding their worth or value."[16]

Muelder finds emergent evolution congenial: "The person thus conceived is both a product of brain and general body evolution and a self-developing reality within an ontological whole . . . within an even larger ecological whole. . . ."[17] "Since time is real, all is process . . ." and "The body of a person as well as the self is involved along with God in this complex process."[18]

For process philosophers who adopt a view of time as a reality rather than, as it is for Aristotle, a product of the mind, the nature of the human being in a world of time will necessarily be different from that seen in Aristotle's philosophy. Thus the importance of time for a study of the human person becomes evident: in a world in which reincarnation is taken for granted, as it is in the Hindu world, for example, the nature of human life and its potential tragedy is quite different from what it is in a world in which a human being is seen as having one life uniquely his or her own.

These considerations of some personalist tenets will serve to show how personalism as a school of thought differs from the point of view adopted by those for whom Aristotle continues to be the "Master of all who know."

NOTES

1. Maurice Nédoncelle, *Vers une Philosophie de l'Amour et de la Personne* (Paris: Aubier, 1957).
2. Nédoncelle, *Toward a Philosophy*, 236–237 (my translation).
3. Ibid., 238–239.
4. Ibid., 257.
5. Ibid., 165.
6. Ibid., 186.
7. Ibid., 222.
8. W. Muelder, "Person as Embedded and Embodied," 1.
9. Ibid., 2.
10. Ibid., 3.
11. Ibid., 26.
12. Ibid.
13. Ibid., 7. P. Teilhard de Chardin often speaks in a panpsychist vein.
14. Ibid., 10.
15. Ibid., 12.
16. Ibid., 15.
17. Ibid., 18.
18. Ibid., 22.

Select Bibliography

BOOKS

Aristotle. *Aristotle's Categories and Propositions*. Edited and translated with a commentary by H. G. Apostle. Grinnell, IA: The Peripatetic Press, 1980.

———. *Aristotle's Nicomachean Ethics*. Edited and translated with a commentary by H. G. Apostle. Grinnell, IA: The Peripatetic Press, 1984.

———. *Aristotle's Politics*. Edited and translated with a commentary by H. G. Apostle. Grinnell, IA: The Peripatetic Press, 1986.

———. *Aristotle's Metaphysics*. Translated with commentaries and glossary by H. G. Apostle. Bloomington: Indiana University Press, 1966.

———. *Aristotle Selected* Works. Translated by H. G. Apostle and Lloyd P. Gerson. Grinnell, IA: The Peripatetic Press, 1982.

Augustine, Saint. *The Trinity*. Washington, DC: The Catholic University of America Press, 1963.

Boethius, Anicius Manlius Severinus. *A Treatise against Eutyches and Nestorius*. In *The Theological Tractates*. Translated by H. F. Stewart and E. K. Rand. New York: G. P. Putnam's Sons, 1926.

Carrithers, Michael, Steven Collins, and Steven Lukes. *The Category of the Person: Anthropology, philosophy, history*. Cambridge: Cambridge University Press, 1985.

Chenu, M.-D. *Nature, Man, and Society in the Twelfth Century: Essays on New Theological Perspectives in the Latin West*. Translated by Jerome Taylor and Lester K. Little. Chicago: The University of Chicago Press, 1963.

Chisholm, Roderick. *Person and Object: A Metaphysical Study*. London: George Allen and Unwin, 1976.

Clarke, W. Norris. *Person and Being*. Milwaukee: Marquette University Press, 1993.

Duns Scotus, John. *God and Creatures: The Quodlibetal Questions*. Translated with an Introduction, Notes, and Glossary by Felix Alluntis and Allan B. Wolter. Princeton: Princeton University Press, 1975.

Gill, Christopher, ed. *The Person and the Human Mind; Issues in Ancient and Modern Philosophy*. Oxford: Clarendon Press, 1990.

Macmurray, John. *Persons in Relation*. Atlantic Highlands, NJ: Humanities Press International, 1991.

———. The Self as Agent. Atlantic Highlands, NJ: Humanities Press International, 1991.

Marcel, Gabriel. *Creative Fidelity*. Translated with an Introduction by Robert Rosthal. New York: Farrar, Straus and Company, 1964.

McCall, Catherine. *The Concept of Person: An Analysis of Concepts of Person, Self, and Human Being*. Brookfield, VT: Gower Publishing Company, 1990.

Nota, John H. *Max Scheler: The Man and His Work*. Translated by Theodore Plantinga and John H. Nota. Chicago: Franciscan Herald Press, 1983.

Owens, Joseph. *The Doctrine of Being in the Aristotelian Metaphysics*. 2nd ed. Toronto: The Pontifical Institute of Mediaeval Studies, 1963.

Peacocke, Arthur, and Grant Gillett, eds. *Persons and Personality: A Contemporary Inquiry*. Oxford: Basil Blackwell, 1987.

Principe, Walter H. *William of Auxerre's Theology of the Hypostatic Union*. Vol. 1 of *The Theology of the Hypostatic Union in the Early Thirteenth Century*. 4 vols. Toronto: The Pontifical Institute of Mediaeval Studies, 1963.

Sahi, Jyoti. *The Child and the Serpent*. London: Routledge and Kegan Paul, 1980.

Strawson, P. F. *Individuals: An Essay in Descriptive Metaphysics*. Garden City, NY: Doubleday & Company, 1963.

Thomas Aquinas, Saint. *On the Power of God*. Translated by the English Dominican Fathers. London: Burns Oates & Washburn, 1934.

———. *Summa Contra Gentiles*. 4 vols. Translated by Charles J. O'Neil. Garden City, NY: Doubleday & Company, 1957.

———. *Summa Theologiae*. Latin text and English translation. 60 vols. Vol. 6, *The Trinity*. Translated by Ceslaus Velecky. New York: McGraw-Hill Book Company, 1964.

Wiggins, David. *Sameness and Substance*. Oxford: Basil Blackwell, 1980.

Wojtyla, Karol. *The Acting Person*. Boston: D. Reidel Publishing Co., 1979.

ARTICLES

Rorty, Amelie O. "Persons and *Personae*." In *The Person and the Human Mind: Issues in Ancient and Modern Philosophy*, edited by Christopher Gill, 21–38. Oxford: The Clarendon Press, 1990.

Teichman, Jenny. "The Definition of *Person*." *Philosophy* 60 (1985): 175–85.

Index

accidental categories, 79–133
accidents, 12, 13, 25, 74–75, 81–84, 93–94
action, 110–16, 136, 137
actor, 63, 71
acts, of person. *See* person, acts of
addiction, 99, 114
Adler, Mortimer, 16n. 14
agency, 4, 18, 83, 84, 91, 135
Allen, Prudence, 106
Allport, Gordon, 18, 19
Anaxagoras, 92
angels, 98, 135
Aquinas, Thomas. *See* Thomas Aquinas, Saint
Aristotle, 46, 72, 75, 87, 102, 141; and Dewey, 20, 26; and passion, 113; and sciences, 95; categories of, 104–9, 119–34, 136; critics of categories, 10–17; ethics in, 94; in medieval thought, 57–60; nature in, 89–96; on having, 129; soul in, 85; substance in, 4, 37, 80; time in, 74; works: *Categories*, 3, 5, 14; *De Anima*, 92; *Metaphysics*, 92, 128; *Nichomachaean Ethics*, 82; *On the Generation of Animals*, 93; *Physics*, 14, 91, 119, 128; *Posterior Analytics*, 25; *Topics*, 128
Arnauld, Antoine, 15n. 6
art and arts, 90, 129, 132, 140
artists, 131
attributes, 45, 137
Augustine, Saint, 29n. 41, 47, 49, 58, 137
Austin, J. L., 112

Bachelard, Gaston, 100
Baier, Annette, 26, 27
Baldwin, James Mark, 21
beauty, 137
being, 61, 136, 137
Berdiaev, N., 139
Bergson, Henri, 119–20

Bhagavad Gita, 6n. 4
body, 56–60, 71, 86, 92, 98, 99, 122, 123, 130
Boethius, 43, 48–49, 63, 74, 84, 89, 98, 135, 136; *Against Eutyches and Nestorius*, 48; definition of person, 1, 3–5, 48, 68, 88n. 10; eighteenth century writers and, 68, 69; medieval philosophers and, 56, 57, 62
"Boston Personalism," 139, 141
Bowne, Borden Parker, 139, 140
Braun, René, 51nn. 16, 18
Brightman, Edgar S., 141
Brockelman, Paul, 121
Buddha, Gautama, 4, 6n. 4, 110–11, 115
Butler, Bishop Joseph, 71

Cajetan, Cardinal Thomas de Vio, 88n. 9
Calvinism, 28n. 25
categories: Aristotelian, 3, 5, 25, 70, 72, 89–109, 137; as manifesting structure of world, 14; as predicaments, 10; critics of, 10–15; Kantian, 38n. 3
causes, 91, 96
change, 31, 74, 82–83, 86, 113, 115, 119, 121
Chantraine, Pierre, 42
charity, 57
Chenu, M.-D., 54
Chesterton, G. K., 10
child, 4, 21, 22, 104, 116
Cicero, 2, 42–45, 48, 49, 76n. 8; *De Officiis*, 48
clothing, 127–33, 140
commitment, 31
confrontation, 31–33, 35
Confucian thought, 81, 82
Confucius, 89, 95
consciousness, 71, 73–74, 107
conservation, 99
contemplation, 121. *See also* mystical experience
contingency, 59

corporate persons, 135
court, 44
Cousins, Ewert, 56, 57

Das, Veena, 130
death, 58, 60, 93, 110, 124, 127
definitions, 13, 94
Deity, 73. *See also* God
democracy, 26
Democritus, 92
depersonalization, Nazi strategy of, 129
Descartes, René, 3, 11, 73, 76n. 13, 81;
    and dichotomy between mind and
    body, 75, 99, 114; *Meditations*, 98
De Smet, Richard, S. J., 50n. 5
Dewey, John, 9, 18–27, 37, 41, 42,
    63, 135; availability of *Encyclopaedia
    Britannica* to, 73, 75; *Corporate
    Personality*, 23; *Freedom and
    Culture*, 26
disposition, 95–96
Divine Persons, 58, 98
Drobner, Hubertus R., 52n. 30

East, action and passion in the, 110–16
Eastern thinkers, 53
Eckhart, Meister, 65n. 32
ecological issues, 106
economics, 106–7, 113, 122, 131
efficient causality, 91, 96
emotions, 96, 116
empathy, 114
Encyclopaedia Britannica, 10; person in,
    67–77
environmental issues, 106
Epictetus, 46
essence, 25, 85–86, 94; Marcel and, 33;
    Thomas Aquinas and, 59, 86. *See also*
    being
ethics, 97n. 18
existence, 56, 59, 86, 113, 122
existentialist philosophy, 36
experience, 21, 54

face, 43, 46, 62–63, 98. *See also*
    prosopon
Fichte, J. G., 30
final cause, 91, 96
Flewelling, R. T., 139
formal cause, 91, 96

freedom, 35, 61, 100, 101, 131
Freud, Sigmund, 112
friendship, 82
funeral customs, 127

Galen, 46
genus, 13, 25, 135
Gill, Christopher, 88n. 10, 100
God, in Boethius's definition, 135; in
    Marcel, 34; in Scotus, 61; in Thomas
    Aquinas, 58, 65n. 23; personalist
    philosophers and, 139, 140, 141
goodness, 137
Gottschalk, H. B., 7n. 13
Gratry, Alphonse, 29n. 41, 52n. 33

habit, 94–95, 127; in Dewey, 18, 21
haecceitas, 61
having, 127–34; and society, 131–32
Hegel, G. W. F., 131; *Phenomenology of
    Mind*, 107
Heidegger, Martin, 35, 66n. 43, 100
Heraclitus, 82, 119
Hindu thought, 81, 122
Hitler, Adolf, 19, 26
Hobbes, Thomas, 11, 53, 62, 135;
    theory of the state, 63
hoc aliquid, 58
Hölscher, Ludger, 47
Hopkins, Gerard Manley, 2, 61, 131
human beings, 54
human nature, 45, 61. *See also* person
human rights, 26, 35, 107
Husserl, Edmund, 105
hypostasis 50n. 6, 59; as person, 37, 45,
    49, 59; in Augustine, 47; in Dewey,
    25; in *Encyclopaedia Britannica*, 71; in
    Leontius of Byzantium, 48

identity, personal, 1, 3, 68–69, 71–72
immortality, personal, 99
Incarnation, doctrine of the, 61; dogma
    of, 86; theology of, 57
individual, 56, 84, 112; contrasted to
    person, 19; in ancient sources, 47, 48;
    in Dewey, 24; in *Encyclopaedia
    Britannica*, 70–71; in John of
    Damascus, 49; in Marcel, 32–33;
    revealed by clothing, 129, 133. *See
    also* person

individuality, in Dewey, 22; in medieval
  sources, 55, 60–61
intention, 109n. 18, 112, 121

Jain monks, nuns, 101
jewelry, 130
John of Damascus, 43, 49, 53
John Paul II, 9. *See also* Wojtyla, Karol
justice, 99

Kant, Immanuel, 4, 19, 22, 76n. 12,
  131; categories of, 11, 38n. 3;
  Critique of Practical Reason, 111
Kantian, 37, 73, 75

Lacroix, J., 139
Lavelle, L., 139
Lavely, J. H., 141
law, 35, 112, 123; English Common
  Law, 107; Roman law, 20, 42
legal rights, 35
Leibniz, Gottfried Wilhelm, 73
leisure, 107, 122
Leontius of Byzantium, 48
Le Senne, R., 139
Locke, John, 4, 25, 61, 82, 98, 135;
  and personal identity, 136; in the
  Encyclopaedia Britannica, 70
Lockean, 37, 68
Luther, Martin, 76n. 8

Macfarquhar, Colin, 70, 76n. 5
Macmurray, John, 4
Marcel, Gabriel, 9, 15, 30–40, 100,
  105, 111, 136, 139
Maritain, Jacques, 118n. 13, 139
Marx, Karl, 107, 113, 122
marxists, 35
mask, as meaning of *persona*, 34, 42–46,
  48, 51n. 14, 63, 70, 73
material cause, 91, 96
memory, 47, 69, 85, 92, 120
Merleau-Ponty, Maurice, 98
metaphysics, 37, 85, 105, 137; as study
  of being, 57; in *Encyclopaedia
  Britannica*, 68–69, 71; Marcel and, 33
Mill, John Stuart, 4, 10–12, 127, 136
Miller, Alice, 108n. 10
mind, 47, 120, 122
morality, 86n. 10, 113, 120, 131

Morris, George, 75
motion, 90
Mounier, Emmanuel, 139
Muelder, Walter, 140
Mühlen, Heribert, 14
mystery, distinction between problem
  and, 36; of human personality, 111;
  of pain, 116
mystical experience, 115

nature, 15, 48, 56, 85–86, 89–96;
  human beings as part of, 54; rational,
  59. *See also* human nature
Nédoncelle, Maurice, 43–46, 139–40
negatives, in Scotus, 62
Nemesius, 43, 49; *On the Nature of
  Man*, 46–47
Neville, Dean Robert C., 141
New Testament, 46
Novak, Michael, 79

O'Hara, M. L., 87n. 7
on (one), 32–33, 35
oneness, 137
Ortega y Gassett, José, 121
ousia, 10, 11, 47, 80, 82

pain, 114–16
Panaetius, 46
Parfit, Derek, 114–15, 124; persons as
  aggregates, 6n. 4
Parmenides, 119
passion, 12, 110–16
person, acts of, 31–32, 37, 43, 72, 74,
  84, 95, 130; agency of, 4, 18, 63,
  111; and God, 34, 55; "artificial"
  person, 63; as an individual substance,
  80–88; as author, 63; as citizen, 25,
  135; as composite of body and soul,
  58–59, 75, 86, 120; as consciousness,
  74–75; as constituted by acts, 72; as
  educable, 34; as end, 22; as *homo
  viator*, 30; as incommunicable, 56, 60,
  63n. 9; as legal agent, 62; as receiver,
  4; as a rational substance, 56, 59 (*see
  also* substance); as a related being, 30,
  62, 86, 104–7; as social, 95, 104,
  106; contrasted to individual, 32, 33;
  definition of, 2, 23, 48, 68, 69;
  dignity of, 36; functional emphasis

with regard to, 135; historicity of, 121; history of the notion of, 41–75; in ancient sources, 42–52; in Buddhism, 6n. 4; in Cicero, 44–55; in the East, 96; in the *Encyclopaedia Britannica*, 67–77; in Greek tradition, 20, 42, 135; in Latin tradition, 42, 135; in Roman law, 20; in society, 4, 21, 25, 113, 131; juridic, 45, 106; justice and, 33; legal functions of, 68, 69; medieval and early modern views of, 53–66; metaphysical reflection on, 34, 68; objections to categorization of, 9–17; objections to traditional notions of, 9–24; Old Testament roots, 42; ontological account of, 79–134; structural emphasis, 135; technical progress and, 34; word 'person', 3–5, 18–19, 41–77

persona, 24, 42–47, 54, 63, 71, 135
personage, 42–44
personal identity. *See* identity, personal
personalisms, 139–42
personality, 2, 6, 15, 43, 45, 49, 60, 102, 111, 131, 136, 137; as completion of person, 58, 120; in Dewey, 18–27; in *Encyclopaedia Britannica*, 68–74; in Marcel, 36–37; in Scotus, 62; legal concept of, 25
personhood, 61, 62; as consciousness, 67
persons, Divine. *See* Divine Persons
phenomenology, 105
physics, 86
Piaget, Jean, 105
Pieper, Josef, 107
place, 100–101, 132, 137, 140
Plato, 81, 85, 92, 113, 119
pleasure, 113–15
Plotinus, 7n. 13, 120
politics, 95
Porphyry, 7n. 13
position, 101–2
possessing. *See* having
possessions, 127–34, 137
potency, 120
potentiality, 86, 92, 119–20
powers, 72, 90, 92–93
predicables, 3, 12–13, 25, 70
predicamentals, 25
predicaments, 10, 12–13, 70, 72, 111

predicates, 12–13, 128, 136–137
Principe, Walter H., 64n. 1
prosopon, 3, 42–46, 62–63, 71, 135
Protestantism, 22
psychotherapy, 115
'*purusa*', 50n. 12
Pythagoreans, 92

quality, 3, 6, 12, 43, 79, 89–96, 137
quantity, 12, 98–99, 137
Quintillian, 50n. 6

rational nature, 59, 68, 89–97
rational psychology, 73
Reid, Thomas, 73
relation, 6, 12, 25, 43, 58, 79, 103n. 12, 136; relationship, 104–9, 123, 137
responsibility, 31–32, 84
rest, 90
Rheinfelder, H., 45
Richard of Saint Victor, 53–60, 62, 104, 136
Ricoeur, Paul, 112, 139
rights, natural, 24. *See also* human rights
Roth, Robert J., 29n. 52
Royce, Josiah, 19, 21, 39n. 46

Sahi, Jyoti, 131
Scheler, Max, 87n.4, 96, 103nn. 12, 13, 105, 136, 139
Schlossman, S., 46
Schmaus, Michael, 14
Schopenhauer, Arthur, 110
science, natural, 81
Scotus, John Duns, 53, 60–62, 86, 136
self, 68
self-consciousness, 43
self-transcendence, 57
Seneca, 50n. 6
Sève, Lucien, 121
slavery, 20, 22
soul, 83, 85–86, 93, 99, 112, 122–23; and nature, 92–93; inadequacy of term for human person, 54–60; in Augustine, 47; in Dewey, 18
space, 119
species, 13
Stein, Edith, 105–6, 114
Stern, W., 139

Stewart, Dugald, 10–12, 63, 72–73
Stough, Charlotte, 16n. 8
Strawson, P. F., 14
structuralism, 112
subsistence, 49, 55, 83–85
substance, 4–6, 10, 37, 80–87, 89, 93–94, 105, 123, 136–37; definition of, in *Categories*, 83; in ancient sources, 43–49; in Aristotle, 12, 14–15; in Dewey, 25; in *Encyclopaedia Britannica*, 68–75; in medieval writings, 55–59; in *Oxford English Dictionary*, 80
substantia, 10, 11, 46
substantiality, 55, 135
suffering, 4, 113–15. *See also* passion

technology, 129, 131
television, 34, 107
Tertullian, 24, 46, 49, 51n. 16
theology, 24, 57, 61
Thomas Aquinas, Saint, 16n. 14, 43, 49, 53, 57–60, 61, 72, 112, 123, 136; *Commentary on the Sentences*, 58; definition of person, 24; essence in, 86; having or possessing in, 129–30;

on personality, 39n. 43; on potency, 120; quantity in, 99; soul in, 85
time, 74, 114–26, 137, 140, 141
torture, 111, 114
totalitarian state, 36, 106
Transcendent, the, 35
transcendentals, 137
Trendelenburg, Adolf, 42, 75
Trinity, theology of the, 57, 86

universals, 53, 81

virtue, 94–95, 128
volition, 74

Wallace, William A., 124
West, action and passion in the, 110–16
"when." *See* time
Whitehead, Alfred North, 81
Wiggins, David, 6n. 4, 99
will, 23
Wojtyla, Karol, 87n. 4, 97n. 5, 105, 136
wonder, 115
work, 122, 131, 132
world, structure of, 14